SAVE

YOURSELF

M000031992

SAVE YOURSELF

Your Guide to Saving for Retirement and Building Financial Security

Julie Grandstaff, CFA

PORTLAND, OREGON

Save Yourself: Your Guide to Saving for Retirement and Building Financial Security
SeSo,LLC, Portland, Oregon
© 2018 by Julie Grandstaff

All rights reserved. Published by SeSo, LLC. No part of this publication may be reproduced or distributed in any form or by any means, or stored in a database or retrieval system, without the prior written permission of the publisher.

Editing and design by Indigo: Editing, Design, and More

ISBN: 978-1-7329341-0-8
LCCN: 2018913789

To my husband, Jeff, without whose encouragement this book would only live on my computer.

Contents

Acknowledgments

A VERY SPECIAL THANK YOU TO MIKE PONDER AND CHERYL De Renzy, who waded through my first horrible draft; to Suzanne Warner, whose valuable feedback made this book far more readable; to Dan Sharp for giving it the once-over with his eagle eyes; and to Jon Woodson for his advice and help in making it a success. Thank you also to all of you who shared your stories and allowed me to poke my nose into your financial lives. Many of those stories are included in these pages. You know who you are. Finally, thank you to the team at Indigo—Kristen Hall-Geisler, Jenn Zaczek, Dehlia McCobb, Vinnie Kinsella, and Olivia Croom—for a beautiful, professional presentation.

Introduction

FINANCIAL SECURITY IS NOT JUST FOR THE LUCKY ONES WHO earn more money than you. In fact, many of them struggle with their finances too. There is no fancy formula or secret investment strategy that somehow you missed. Your financial security boils down to one simple thing: how much you save.

This book is about helping you understand why and how much you should be saving, and it will show you how to get on track. It focuses on saving for retirement but demonstrates how to save for all your financial goals. You'll learn how you can take control and have the financial security you need both now and later in life.

Americans are not saving enough to support themselves when they retire, and many are just one setback away from financial disaster. You may have seen the statistics. Reports highlighting America's dismal finances are commonplace. Here are a few:

- Sixty-nine percent of Americans have less than $1,000 in savings[1]
- The median 401(k) balance is $24,713[2]
- The average household credit card balance is $15,654[3]

But we really shouldn't be surprised by this pervasive financial insecurity. In a single generation, there has been a dramatic shift in all things financial. Employers no longer provide for our income in our old age. The cost of a college education is almost five times higher than it was thirty years ago, resulting in mountains of student loan debt. Borrowing money—once mostly for large, infrequent purchases like a home or car—is now done for everything, including the morning latte. We were not prepared for such a dramatic change.

If you are worried about money and your future, you are not alone. If the statistics above sound like you, you have good reason to be worried. But the fact that you haven't mastered your finances yet doesn't mean you aren't capable of doing it now.

Save Yourself has three sections. The first three chapters are devoted to helping you understand why as a society America hasn't mastered saving, the psychological barriers that keep you from saving, and why everyone needs to save.

Then the book walks you through setting goals with a focus on the ones that everyone should have, assessing your situation, developing a strategy for meeting your goals, and reviewing your progress. It stresses the need to define what is important to you so that you can minimize spending on things that are unimportant. This section of the book also illustrates how to calculate the dollar value of your goals with step-by-step instructions and examples in worksheets. It covers the different types of debt and how they work as well as the best approaches to pay off those debts. In addition, it walks you through common setbacks and how to deal with them.

The last section of the book covers investments and end-of-life documents and insurance. Starting with investment fundamentals, you will learn how investments work so you can become a better consumer of advice and products. Straightforward approaches to having your savings invested for you are explained. Then *Save Yourself* covers setting up a will, figuring out if you need life insurance, designating beneficiaries, and putting other end-of-life documents in place.

The final chapter brings all these concepts together. It follows a couple as they create their own financial plan through weekly activities. It uses step-by-step worksheets to calculate the dollar value of the couple's goals and creates a plan that allows them to save an emergency fund, contribute to their retirement plans, and pay off debt. In addition, they set up their family for continued success if one or both should pass away unexpectedly.

By the time you finish the book, you will be able to create your own financial plan. Fair warning: there is math involved, but it's nothing you can't handle. Wherever a calculation is necessary, you will find references to online tools that will do the work for you. In each chapter, the main ideas are summarized at the end. If there are words or phrases you might not know, they are defined. You'll see these in bold throughout the chapters, and the definitions are also summarized at each chapter's end. This allows you to easily find concepts if you want to revisit what you read.

No question about it—taking control of your financial future is hard work. You'll start making choices you may have avoided up until now. If you are like most, nothing has prepared you to take control of your financial life. But if you've picked up this book, you are probably ready to do just that. You already have the skills you need. You just need a little help in applying them.

I spent my career in the investment management industry, much of it helping companies choose investments for their

retirement savings plans. While the clients were mainly concerned with the investments, their employees had so little saved
that it made little difference what investments they chose. The
average account balance wouldn't be nearly enough to pay the
bills in retirement.

I have seen firsthand what it's like to not have enough money
to pay the bills. My mother has lived solely on Social Security
for years, since arthritis made it difficult for her to work. Until
recently, she lived in an aging trailer park near the Mexico border.
The pad rent was low, and my brother bought the used trailer for
her for less than the cost of a car. She had enough for the basics
and to keep up her crafting but nothing more. A problem with her
trailer or her car was simply something she couldn't afford to fix.
Even that lifestyle was only possible due to the low cost of living
in that area. It would have been impossible in most US cities.

Even before this, Mom's life was not easy. She raised four kids
mostly on her own. We didn't have a lot of money when we were
growing up. But she had opportunities to be more financially
secure. Among the lean times, there were times when she was
relatively flush. But her spending rose and fell with her income,
leaving nothing saved for emergencies let alone retirement.

That does not have to be you. It wasn't me. My husband and
I retired in our fifties with enough money to provide the lifestyle
we planned. We did it by knowing our goals and priorities and
saving enough to make them happen.

Since leaving work, I have helped dozens of people understand their own financial situation and create a plan for the future.
It is their stories you will see interwoven through the book. Some
of the tales are cautionary, and some are triumphant. All are real.
Perhaps one of their stories will ring true with you, and the related advice will help you move forward.

Imagine the feeling of peace you will have knowing that you have enough money to manage a medical emergency or a short time out of work. Or the confidence you will have with money set aside to pursue your dreams. Or the satisfaction you will have knowing when you can stop working for pay and how you will live when you do.

Financial stress is bad for your health. It can lead to anxiety, depression, and even physical pain. But you can eliminate it by taking the steps, following the examples, and working through the worksheets provided in this book. Yes, simply knowing what you will do and how you will do it goes a long way toward making you feel more secure. Then, when you are successful, you can even feel a little smug if you want.

There is no time like the present to make the changes necessary to secure your financial future. The longer you wait, the fewer choices you have and the harder it becomes. Starting now, from wherever you are, will give you the most opportunities to control your own destiny. Read on and learn how to save yourself.

PART 1

Chapter 1

The Rise and Fall of Retirement

EACH OF US HAS A VISION FOR RETIREMENT. WE HAVE A SPECIFIC idea about how we want to live that is unique to us, and we have this vision where we have the time and money to do what we want for many years without working for pay. That ideal is based on lifestyles largely funded by employer-provided pension plans.

But pensions barely exist any longer. Instead our employers are offering us retirement savings plans that have several advantages, but they're lacking the guaranteed income provided by a traditional pension. We must figure out how to support ourselves for potentially decades on our own savings and investments.

It is becoming increasingly clear that we haven't adapted well to the shift from pensions to savings plans. Despite the loss of this safety net, Americans are saving less than ever. The Employee Benefit Research Institute estimates that more than four in ten of us won't be able to pay for our basic needs let alone fund the idyllic retirement we've come to expect. How did we get here?

What the Heck Is Retirement?
Retirement wasn't always a thing. It wasn't until the 1950s that enough companies offered pension benefits to create an expectation for a few years of leisure after a life of work. Before that,

most people simply worked until they couldn't and then relied on their families or communities for support.

Prior to the turn of the twentieth century, most families lived off the land and took care of each other. It was a hard life that took its toll on the very young and the very old. But you could grow or hunt for the food that you needed, and land was cheap. Money was less important than fertile soil and good weather.

As you grew older, you simply continued to work the land. At some point your eldest son might take over the farm and much of the hard work. But you stayed on and did what work you could, from light farm duties to helping to raise the grandkids.

As the American population migrated to the cities, money became more important. With no land to produce food, the only way to make a living was to work for pay. Work was manual and physically difficult in the early years of the twentieth century. You needed a strong back and stamina to survive a day in a factory job. As you got older, it was just harder to do the work, but you still had to work to live. Maybe you took a job that was less physically demanding for less money, but you still worked.

This was a problem for employers who needed more strong, young workers and fewer old ones. In fact, William Osler, a leading thinker and prominent physician of the day, believed, as did others, that after age sixty, people were pretty much useless in terms of being productive members of the workforce.[4]

One new idea for getting older workers out of the workplace was to provide them with enough pay that they could survive without a job. At the end of the 1800s, the first pension plans were born. They gave you a monthly benefit based on your pay and came to be known as **defined benefit pension plans**.

Railroads were among the first to offer pension plans, followed by universities. Public utilities weren't far behind, and by the 1920s retirement benefits had spread to other industries, such as banking and insurance. Larger cities offered pension plans to city workers, police, and firefighters.[5] But it would take a while before they provided much financial security.

A study by the New York Commission on Aging published in 1930 found that 44 percent of people in New York over the age of sixty-five were self-supporting, primarily through work, and more than half were dependent on family and friends.[6] Statistics varied in different communities, but if you weren't working, you were relying on your relatives and your community.

Securing the Seniors

The Great Depression, which lasted from 1929 to 1939, was devastating for many and more so for the elderly. While the unemployment rate for the under-sixty-five set was just over 25 percent, for those over the age of sixty-five, eight in ten were out of work. Many of those who had pensions lost them when businesses collapsed.[7] With more of the elderly unable to support themselves, pressure to provide some form of government support was growing.

Other countries, primarily in Europe, had already put public retirement systems in place, beginning with Germany in 1889. In the United States, Franklin Delano Roosevelt initiated the Social Security Act, which was passed in 1935.[8] The Social Security system was considered one of the crowning government achievements of the century.

The implementation of Social Security sparked an explosion in the creation of private pension plans. The Committee on Economic Security, which developed the Social Security Act, stated that reaching a retirement income level near 50 percent of a worker's previous average earnings was "socially desirable."[9]

This became a benchmark for pension benefits. With the advent of Social Security, it became less costly for companies to offer pensions that, together with Social Security, met the 50 percent earnings replacement goal.

By 1950, 25 percent of the private workforce was covered by a pension plan.[10] Add to that government employees covered by pensions, and a substantial part of the workforce could look forward to an income after they stopped working.

Combined with Social Security, the promise of a pension benefit made a secure retirement—where you didn't have to work or live with your kids—possible. Best of all, you didn't have to even think about it beyond sticking with your job long enough to collect.

The wave of pension creations continued through the 1970s. The combination of Social Security and pension plan benefits vastly improved the economic security of the elderly. By the mid-1970s, the poverty rate among the elderly had dropped to just 15 percent, half of what it was fifteen years prior.[11]

The Beginning of the End of Pension Plans

It was the golden age of pension plans, and it was coming to an end. Regulations and a new government focus on revenue lost to tax-exempt retirement plans chipped away at the foundations of the defined benefit system. They ultimately led to the decline of company-funded pensions.

The First Blow

The first blow was regulatory. The Employee Retirement Income Security Act (ERISA) was enacted in 1974. While the law made great strides in ensuring that pension coverage was fair and equitable and benefits would actually be paid, it inadvertently created an incentive for companies to move away from defined benefit plans.

The law limited the amount of pension benefits that could be paid out. Higher-paid employees, mostly executives, could not have the same income replacement ratio from the pension as lower-paid employees with these caps.

So companies began providing supplemental **defined contribution plans** to help higher-paid employees make up for the cap on their pension benefits. Defined contribution plans only promise the return of the contributions and whatever investment return they earn instead of a monthly guaranteed payment in retirement, as is the case with defined benefit plans.

In the late 1970s, the government also created section 401(k) of the tax code, which allowed workers to voluntarily contribute a part of their salary pretax to employer-sponsored savings or profit sharing plans. 401(k) plans were a lower-cost and seemingly reasonable alternative to traditional defined benefit plans. They proved to be wildly popular, and growth in 401(k) plans and other defined contribution plans ballooned.[12]

The Second Blow

In the early 1980s, new accounting rules came out requiring plan sponsors to fund pensions as they were earned instead of funding the full projected benefit across a worker's career. That meant contributions for younger workers would be lower than if companies simply funded the retirement equally every year. As workers got closer to retirement, contributions would be higher.

Then in 1987, in an attempt to shore up tax revenue without increasing tax rates, Congress adopted new rules designed to limit the tax sheltering offered by pension plans. The rules reduced the amount of pension funding that could be deducted for tax purposes to less than what was necessary to fully fund the pension obligations.

The result of the new accounting and tax rules combined was a virtual requirement to substantially underfund pension benefits early in a worker's career. This was great for employers as long as their employees were young. The problem came when a large proportion of workers approached retirement age. Then the cost of providing the benefit would explode.[13]

The Final Blow

The final blow came when the tech bubble burst and stock markets declined from 2000 to 2002. Previously the growing level of pension underfunding had been hidden. Gains in the investment markets in the late 1980s and through the 1990s caused pensions to look flush. That allowed businesses to reduce contribution rates and still maintain a fully funded status per the regulatory requirements.

But the stock market decline revealed the cracks in the system. Over this three-year period, the Dow Jones Industrial Average lost more than 38 percent of its value. At the same time, those workers who had been in the early stages of their careers in the mid-1980s were far closer to retirement and collecting their pension benefits at this point. That meant the costs to fund their retirements grew rapidly.

The combination of weak investment markets and increased funding costs for older employees resulted in big gaps in overall pension funding and large increases in funding expenses for most pension plans. Defined benefit plans began dropping like flies. By 2010, only 14 percent of the private-sector workforce was covered by a defined benefit pension plan, down from a peak of 45 percent.[14]

Not only are corporate pensions now disappearing, but state and local government pensions are in dire straits as well. On average, municipal pensions are underfunded by 26 percent, and of the fifty largest US cities, twenty won't be able to pay their pension obligations by 2025.[15] Pension benefits are being reduced for those newer to government jobs.

We Should Have Seen It Coming:
The Demise of Social Security

Now we are seeing that Roosevelt's crowning achievement is on uncertain footing as well. Social Security benefit payments have exceeded tax receipts into the program since 2010. The Social Security Trust Funds will be able to fund this deficit through 2034, but after that, the assets will be exhausted.[16] If changes aren't made to the system, the government simply won't be able to make the benefit payments as promised.

When Social Security was proposed, Roosevelt envisioned a program that would be self-funding. Contributions for a worker would be collected over his or her lifetime and invested. The contributions and investment interest combined would provide the funding to pay out the worker's benefit at the end of their work life.

Of course, that wasn't possible in the early years of the program because it would be decades before a worker would have contributed enough for a fully funded benefit. Therefore, the early payments had to be funded from the contributions of those still working. The new law included a schedule of tax increases to be implemented over time to make the program self-funding. Without the tax increases, the system was projected to require government subsidization by 1980.[17]

Unfortunately, subsequent amendments to the law repeatedly pushed back the tax increases, making the program a

pay-as-you-go system. Pay-as-you-go systems rely on revenue from those still working to pay for the benefits of retirees. They become extremely expensive as more people begin receiving benefits.

When Social Security was implemented, the benefit payments were cheap relative to the tax revenues that were being collected. In 1940, there were more than 159 workers for every beneficiary. Now the ratio is less than three to one.

Social Security has been rescued twice: once in 1977 and again in 1982. The second fix took nearly two decades to implement and pushed the full retirement age out to sixty-seven.[18] Now the system needs a third fix.

The 1982 fix was intended to secure financing for Social Security for the coming seventy-five years up to 2058. The projections were wrong. Low interest rates and the wave of baby boomers retiring have shortened the time to the next funding crisis to 2034, at which point trust fund assets will be exhausted. Without assets to redeem, the system will be solely dependent on tax revenues, and revenue for the program will only be able to fund about three-quarters of currently promised benefits.[19]

The only conclusion to be drawn is that another overhaul is on the horizon. Future benefits will have to be lowered in some way. Tax increases alone would likely be too large for the working public to swallow. The cost of the program is expected to rise to nearly 17 percent of workers' taxable earnings by 2038.[20]

The possible methods for reducing benefits include pushing back the age where a person can receive full benefits further from the current age of sixty-seven, taxing more of the Social Security benefit, and simply outright reducing the benefit. Regardless of the method, it means less income from Social Security for future retirees.

With fewer people able to collect pensions and the prospect of Social Security benefits shrinking, we are left to our own devices to figure out how to make ends meet once we stop working. But after a history of retirees getting their retirement income handed to them with little effort on their part, we've lost the knowledge and skills to do it ourselves.

For the decades beginning in 1950, 1960, and 1970, the average annual **personal savings rate** was around 10 percent of income. The personal savings rate is the percentage of income left over after spending and taxes. The decade of the 1980s saw a drop in that rate to just over 9 percent, and the 1990s saw a further drop to less than 7 percent. The first decade of the new millennium brought a personal savings rate of less than 5 percent.[21]

The Employee Benefit Research Institute estimates that more than 40 percent of us will not be able to meet average basic and health care expenses in retirement.[22] That statistic doesn't speak to the number of people who will have to pare back their lifestyle even if they can cover basic expenses.

Can We Go Back?

We've developed a cultural expectation of financial security in retirement. Seniors living in poverty are currently seen as the exception and not the rule. Only 15 percent of those over the age of sixty-five live on less than the Census Bureau's Supplemental Poverty Measure.[23]

But looks can be deceiving. Nearly half (45 percent) live on incomes just two times the Supplemental Poverty Measure. The basics may be covered, but it is far from what we've come to expect in retirement. And poverty rates increase with age.[24]

Are we returning to life as it was in the 1920s, where we work until we can't and then rely on the kindness of our families? That may not work out well.

The advice we see most often is that if we haven't saved enough, we need to work longer. Most proposals for fixing Social Security rely on a later retirement date. On the surface, that seems reasonable. We are living longer than we did in the 1920s. Today the average life expectancy is seventy-nine,[25] and if you live to be sixty-five, you can expect to live about nineteen additional years.[26] Moreover, work is less physically demanding than it was in the 1920s.

Many people are working longer. The low point for the number of people over age sixty-four in the workforce came in 1985, with just over one in ten working. At the end of 2014, nearly one in five was working.[27]

But not all the jobs are less physically demanding. A 2010 study by the Center for Economic Policy and Research found that nearly half of older workers were in physically demanding jobs or jobs with difficult working conditions.[28]

We also can't count on being able to work beyond the "normal" retirement date. One third of the people over sixty-four who were not in the labor force at the end of 2017 were disabled.[29] While some people love their work and wouldn't give it up for the world, many find working into their late sixties and early seventies to be taxing and difficult even if they are healthy.

And it is harder to get a job after you turn sixty-four. In a recent study by the National Bureau of Economic Research, applicants age sixty-four to sixty-six received 35 percent fewer callbacks than younger workers with similar qualifications. Women in that age bracket received 47 percent fewer callbacks.[30]

The other side of the support system for the elderly prior to Social Security and pensions was the family, but today it has become relatively uncommon for families to care for their elders. At the turn of the twentieth century, about 57 percent of those

Alma

My great-grandmother Alma Grady came of age in the roaring twenties. She was an independent woman. Of course, she was married. In fact, she was married five times. She was the very picture of the 1920s flapper. She wore makeup and bobbed her hair. She donned short skirts, drank, smoked, and said whatever was on her mind.

And she worked her entire life. When times were tough, she relied on her close friends, and at the end of her life, her family took care of her.

Alma worked for the Rice Hotel in Houston, Texas, all her adult life. She was a waitress for most of her career, but in her sixties, she took a step back and became a hostess. She lived with her dear friend Julia following the end of her last marriage.

Working in the hotel industry, she did not have a pension. But she was thinking about how she would support herself when she stopped working. To provide for her future, she did what many without pensions did in the day. In the 1930s she began buying into an annuity, an insurance policy that would one day pay monthly benefits in retirement. She scraped together twenty-four dollars every month to add to her policy.

Alma finally retired from the Rice Hotel in 1975 at the age of seventy-one. She had her monthly annuity benefit, which amounted to $120, and she received Social Security. Fortunately, life living with her friend Julia was cheap, and she thought she would be okay. She had a stroke within a week of leaving work and came to live with us for a time before dying a couple of years later.

She worked until she couldn't any more. The hotel was closing, and who was going to hire a seventy-one-year-old woman? She relied on her family to take care of her in the short time remaining after retirement.

over sixty-four lived with family. In 2008, while about 16 percent of the population lived in a multigenerational household—one with at least two generations of adults—only about 7 percent of the over-sixty-five population lived in a household where they were not the head of that household. When older people live with their families, they are usually supporting their other family members, not the other way around.

Today, more than a quarter of the sixty-five and over set lives alone, compared to just over one in twenty in 1900.[31] While most Americans believe it is their responsibility to take in aging parents if their parents want to live with them, a sizeable minority of almost four in ten said it was not.

Not enough people will be able to work long enough to hold off poverty in their lives. At the rate we are going, living longer will mean living longer in poverty. While some will be able to live with families, for too many that won't be possible. The only solution is for Americans to understand that we are on our own for funding our financial security in our old age.

There isn't currently a single path to learn how to fund your own retirement. Parents, who are struggling themselves to figure out how to fund a retirement, are not passing skills on to their children. Basic personal financial habits, such as budgeting, saving, and managing debt, get little attention in today's school system. So there isn't any wonder that the generations that started their careers in the 1980s and later with only 401(k) plans for retirement savings will shortly be retiring without enough money to maintain their standard of living or possibly even meet basic expenses.

There is certainly enough information available. Maybe too much. There is advice ranging from how to create a budget to how to become a millionaire. It is wide ranging and often contradictory. To figure it out on your own can be overwhelming.

There are other hurdles to overcome as well. Humans have a natural tendency to prefer immediate gratification to delayed gratification, and Americans have created a culture of consumption. In addition to developing the skills, we need to value our future financial security as well as what our money can buy today

It is possible to attain the financial security you want and need without a pension. Managing your own personal retirement can be boiled down to manageable concepts that anyone can learn. If you are willing to do the work, that financial security can be yours.

Vocabulary

Defined benefit pension plan: A retirement benefit funded by an employer. Payments in retirement are guaranteed by the employer and are based on a formula related to the employee's salary (usually in the final years of work), their time with the company, and their age. Payments may be made monthly, as a lump sum, or a combination of the two, depending on the plan designed by the employer.

Defined contribution plan: A retirement benefit where a portion of the employee's salary is set aside as savings for retirement. The contribution may be made by the employer, the employee, or both.

The balance available for retirement is dependent on the amount of the contributions made and the investment earnings on those contributions.

The most well-known defined contribution plan is the 401(k) plan, but profit sharing plans and stock bonus plans are also defined contribution plans. In addition, government and charitable organizations have their own versions of the 401(k) plan, called 403(b) plans and 457 plans.

Pay-as-you-go system: A retirement system where the contributions from current workers are used to pay the benefits for current retirees.

Personal savings rate: The percentage of income that is not spent or paid in taxes.

Main Ideas

1. Pensions and Social Security made an independent life beyond work possible.
2. By the 1970s, a large portion of the workforce was participating in a pension from their employer, which made planning and saving for retirement unnecessary.
3. Few employers still provide a pension plan. Only 14 percent of today's private-sector workforce will retire with a pension.
4. After years of expanding Social Security, the system is on shaky ground. By 2034, the Social Security trust funds will be depleted, and benefits will depend solely on revenue collected from Social Security taxes. Revenue will only cover about three-quarters of currently promised benefits.
5. Most of us are responsible for our own retirements, yet we are ill prepared.

Chapter 2

Saving Is Hard, but You Can Learn

IT HAS BEEN A RELATIVELY SHORT TIME SINCE WE BEGAN THE shift away from our employers doing the saving and investing for us to us being responsible for figuring it out on our own. Now with almost two-thirds of workers ages fifty-five and older having less than $100,000 in total retirement savings, which isn't nearly enough to cover basic expenses, we are just beginning to understand that we are largely unprepared to take on the task.

Saving is learned. There are a variety of natural human traits that work against us saving for our future. We must build the skills to overcome these tendencies and adequately prepare for the time when we won't be earning a paycheck.

Yet we are reluctant to discuss money issues. Many parents don't share their experiences, situations, and lessons learned with their children. Personal finance is not taught in most public schools, and employers don't talk about how to manage money so staff will have some to contribute to retirement savings plans.

Humans can take incredibly complex activities and reduce them to automatic habits, and people in other countries are saving, which demonstrates that saving for the future is possible. With no formal process for learning the fundamentals, we must overcome some basic human instincts and educate ourselves.

Humans: Naturally Irrational

While we like to believe that we make decisions rationally, there isn't much evidence that it's true. Yet we tend to hang a lot on that assumption.

In the world of economic theory, people make rational choices. According to these theories, saving for the future translates to the idea that whatever an individual has saved is what they should have saved. Even if you are not saving enough to maintain your standard of living after you stop working, it's a rational choice that you might reasonably make so you can maximize your happiness. Rational reasons to not save enough to support your lifestyle might include a belief that a lower standard of living in the future is fine because you will have lived to the fullest today. Or maybe you've decided to pay back your children by becoming a burden on them. Whatever the reason, economic theory assumes that the amount of savings you have is there by your own design.

Culturally, we buy into this theory of rational behavior and value self-sufficiency. There are few better heroes than those who have pulled themselves up by their bootstraps out of a life of poverty to become successful and wealthy. The idea that nobody can take better care of us than we can has driven many of our social policies.

The migration from defined benefit pension plans to defined contribution plans like the 401(k) and its cousins was sold to workers on the idea that we are better off taking care of ourselves. Theoretically, if workers are given an economic incentive, in the form of a tax break, and information about available investments, we will do what is right for ourselves.

Proposals to privatize Social Security are based on the same thing. Let us be responsible for our own outcomes, and the outcomes will be better than what the government can provide.

The fact that very few have a background in pension finance or investing doesn't seem to register as a possible obstacle. Nor does the host of studies that indicate behaving rationally is among the last of the things we should expect from humans.

Human beings simply don't fit the model that economic theory has created, and America's paltry savings is evidence that we can't assume that we do. The following sections highlight how you might fool yourself into thinking you are doing the right thing when you are not.

Who Will You Be in the Future?

It is hard to reconcile the sacrifice of giving up spending today so you can keep spending at a comfortable rate after you stop working.[32] It is hard to translate the amount of money that you are spending into some amount of future income, and even if you could do that, the value of that future income pales in comparison to the joy you believe you will get from spending today.

To illustrate, focus on a single thing, like a vacation. You know that if you take a trip to Hawaii, it will make you very happy. But what if you didn't take the trip today? What if instead you were offered a much lower price on the trip if you put it off for ten years.

You may find it hard to care about the trip ten years from now. A trip today seems like a better choice. What if you're not around to take the trip, or you don't like to travel in the future? What if Hawaii isn't a desirable destination in ten years? If you're going to Hawaii, you want to go soon.

The same principle applies to saving for the future. You know you need to do it, but spending today is more compelling than saving for spending in the future. Why is it so hard to bridge the gap between today and tomorrow?

Studies have shown that you probably don't have any connection to your future self. You don't feel like you know that person who wants to go to Hawaii in ten years, and you certainly don't like the way she looks in a swimsuit. You feel about as close to your future self as you do to a different person altogether.

When you imagine pain or happiness years from now, you imagine it less vividly or believe that somehow it will be less real than what you experience today.[33] Therefore you can't clearly imagine the importance of something that is good for your future self. Saving for the future may feel like choosing between spending today on yourself and giving money to the guy living down the street—not the one who lives there now, whom you know and like, but the guy who will live there years from now.[34]

Researchers at Stanford University, in a study on this relationship, presented study participants with a questionnaire designed to quantify how similar and connected participants felt to themselves in the present versus ten years in the future. In an exercise where the participants were asked to choose between larger delayed prizes and smaller immediate prizes, undergraduates who identified better with their future self were more likely to choose the larger delayed prize.

The researchers took the same questionnaire to subjects in the general community. The participants in this part of the study were also asked about their personal financial situation including their assets, debts, and income. Those participants who identified with their future selves had more accrued assets than those who did not, even controlling for age and income.[35]

If you feel as if you know and like the you of the future, you are more likely to want to take care of that person. Can you change how you feel about your future self? To determine whether help in imagining your future self would make the future more real, and therefore influence you to save more, a different team of researchers presented study participants with a realistically aged picture of themselves. They conducted a series of tests that ended with a simulation of how saving more in the present would increase the subjects' future income. In all the tests, having the image of their gray-haired and wrinkled future in front of them helped the participants feel more connected with the older version of themselves.

These participants were more likely to choose options that had a payoff in the future over a payoff in the present. In the retirement savings simulation, the researchers found that those who saw their older selves allocated more money to retirement savings than those who did not see an aged picture of themselves.[36]

You may not be able to easily simulate how you will age, but you can imagine it. Simply spending time consciously thinking about yourself years in the future can build a better connection to that you. You can also talk to older people you know, like your parents and grandparents, or perhaps elderly neighbors.

1. Ask how your parents or older neighbors are paying for their lifestyle and what they did to get where they are.
2. Try to visualize your life in the future. How do you look? How is your health? Where do you live? Who is in your life?
3. Next think about the future that you want. How do you want to live, and does that line up with the life you're setting up for yourself with your actions today?

The new perspective you draw from contemplating how you will deal with aging and how others have dealt with it may make taking care of the future you more tangible.

Shiny and New: Novelty, an Obstacle to Saving

Saving for the future is an act of smoothing out the ups and downs of our lifestyle over time. But the cost of our lifestyle can be inflated by another one of our many irrational behaviors. We have a natural tendency to buy things that we don't need.

We are the perfect consumers. We have a basic need for novelty and new experiences, but we adapt to our current situations quickly. This need for novelty has been tested and verified across species lines, from humans—adults, children, and infants—to other mammals, including apes, dogs, cats, and rats. When we are first introduced to something new, it makes us happy. But as we are exposed to it for a time, we get used to it, and it no longer brings us pleasure. In fact, we may come to dislike it at some point.[37]

Unlike our furry friends, humans come with a wallet and credit cards, so our need for a new experience often manifests itself in buying stuff. We may buy things simply because we are bored with what we have. Who hasn't bought something new even though you already have something like it that works perfectly well?

This can be relatively small things, like clothes or shoes or golf clubs, but this need for novelty can get much more expensive. Perhaps it's a new car every few years for that new-car smell, or maybe it's a frequent desire to redecorate your home.

Evidence that we buy a lot of things we don't need lies in statistics from the self-storage business. The industry revenue is over $22 billion per year on 2.3 billion square feet of space.[38] That is 7.2 square feet for every man, woman, and child in the United States. Do you really need something if it's in storage?

If to buy is human, how can you resist? What you need is a buzzkill. The next time you get the urge to buy something new, ask yourself the following questions. Chances are if you don't really need whatever it is, these questions will smudge the shine right off it and let you walk by.

- What will you not buy if you buy this? You only have so much money, so something will be set aside, even if it's something in the future.
- Do you already have something like it?
- If so, what's wrong with that?
- How many times will you use it?
- What is the cost per use? Do this math: price divided by the number of times you will use your new thing.

Gratitude for what you already have is also a good antidote for a need for novelty. In *The Paradox of Choice*, author Barry Schwartz suggests practicing gratitude to help you remain content with what you have.[39] If you are shopping for the joy of it, consider the words of interfaith scholar and Benedictine monk David Steindl-Rast: "It is not joy that makes us grateful; it is gratitude that makes us joyful."[40]

Gotta Have It: Temptation and Habits

Much of our behavior is automatic. It is a talent we have developed so we can conserve energy. Conscious thought is an energy drain. If we can accomplish a task without putting much thought into it, it leaves our brain free to do other things. Our conscious self can only do one thing at a time, so if we're distracted by something, our automatic behaviors tend to kick in.

Have you ever gone to the grocery store when you were hungry? If so, you may have noticed that your grocery bill is higher on those days even if you didn't find yourself standing in the

checkout line handing over a half-eaten bag of chips for the ca-
shier to scan. Or maybe after a hard day at work, you bought
those cute strappy sandals even after you promised yourself no
more shopping this month. Under stressful or distracting circumstances, it is much harder to make decisions that are good
for you but involve sacrifice.

What causes this? French scientists have found that under
stress an enzyme attacks a synaptic regulatory molecule in the
brain. As a result, fewer neural connections are made, and we
think less clearly.[41] Whether we're hungry, stressed by work, or
caught up by the excitement of the moment, we are physically less
able to make good decisions. If we are hungry, we are less likely
to choose the carrot sticks over the cookies. If we are stressed
out, we are more likely to give in to temptation. We are wired
to sacrifice our long-term goals for immediate satisfaction. Our
judgment in these circumstances is literally impaired.

Temptation and habits are related. Giving in to temptation can
create new habits. Neuroscientists have found that repeating a
pattern just a few times actually changes our brains. It essentially
establishes new tracks, making it easier for us to travel that line
again in the future. An automatic behavior—or in other words,
a habit—has been created.[42]

For example, one morning you are dragging yourself to work,
and you stop at a local coffee shop for a boost to get you through
until lunch. Maybe it's a tough week, and you do it again on
Friday. Before long, you are stopping every morning even though
you have a coffee maker at home. You may have created a habit,
which can develop without you even knowing about it. They are
formed when a consistent cue leads to a consistent reward after
following a routine.[43] In this case, your cue is the coffee shop

sign or maybe the whiff of fresh coffee as you walk toward your office. Your reward is a boost from the caffeine, and the routine is buying coffee on the way to work. The tracks for a new habit have been laid.

This may play out in any number of ways that can cause you to spend money mindlessly. Whether it's buying your morning coffee at Starbucks, continuing to pay for premium cable channels you don't watch, or maintaining the gym membership where you never work out, mindless spending habits get in the way of your ability to save.

To overcome mindless spending, try being mindful. Mindfulness is being fully present in what you are doing. Being conscious of your actions takes you out of the realm of habitual behavior and into that of your decision-making self.

Start by paying attention when you are about to spend money. Pay with cash instead of a credit or debit card. The tangible reduction of money in your wallet will make you far more conscious of what you're spending than swiping a card.

Try tracking your spending for a week or longer to see exactly how much you are spending and on what. While you may know roughly how much you need to spend, that number is likely to be short of what you actually spend. Many are surprised by the amount of money they spend when they track all their transactions.

Simply knowing where your money is going won't necessarily fix the problem. You can't derail a habit simply by being conscientious. The most effective way to derail a habit is to make it impossible to perform what you do so easily and automatically. One way to minimize mindless spending is to avoid having money on you when you don't have a specific purpose for it. Another strategy is to set up automatic savings deposits from your paycheck or bank account so the money isn't available to you as easily.

Take a break from browsing internet retail outlets. If you get emails with special offers from them, unsubscribe. Go shopping online or in person only when you have a specific need.

Creating a new automatic behavior to take the place of the one you're trying to overcome is also effective. For the coffee example, you might develop a habit of making coffee and taking it with you in an insulated container. If you have coffee with you when you pass the coffee place on the way to work, you aren't likely to step in and buy more. Do this a few times, and you'll have a new habit that costs a lot less.

Keeping Up with the Kardashians

We have an evolutionary need for status. In the animal kingdom, your status in your community determines the order in which you get to eat, how much food you have, and whether you can mate and pass on your genes.

As we've evolved, we've held on to this instinct. We are constantly comparing ourselves to our peers. Our level of satisfaction is based in part on a comparison of what we have to what others like us have.[44] Much of our social life is driven by a desire to be a "big fish."[45]

We have some notion of how a person like us lives, which can drive our decisions about our neighborhood, the type of house in which we live, and the type of car we drive. In our world of constant access to entertainment, news, and information, how we perceive our rank in our community can become distorted. The lifestyles of our favorite characters on TV can be far above what families in similar income brackets can really afford. Those big rooms and high ceilings are more conducive to good camera shots than portraying real life.

Sharon

After Sharon's kids finished elementary school, she figured she was safe to upgrade her home. She had been waiting until they got out of the stage where stains were a given. She put hardwood in the living room and new carpet in the bedrooms. Then it was time to tackle the kitchen.

The 1970s-vintage kitchen certainly needed a face-, as well as a function-, lift. It had flickering fluorescent lighting, chipped tile counters, and an oven that only worked when it wanted. Inspired by her favorite magazine, *Architectural Digest*, and her friends' custom homes, Sharon went all out with the best-of-the-best materials. Her new kitchen had quartz counters, cork flooring, hardwood cabinets—the works. All in, the remodel cost her about $47,000. According to HomeAdvisor.com, that was at the top end of remodeling costs in 2017.[46]

All the finishes were high end. One feature of Sharon's remodel was a professional six-burner, dual-oven stainless steel range that was roughly ten times the cost of a more standard model. Like many of her other choices, this one was a clear status pick.

What makes it a status pick? Sharon didn't cook. An ordinary range would have been more than she needed to support her warm-food needs.

Sharon couldn't finish her kitchen completely as she hoped. She had planned to add additional cabinetry but decided to put that on hold as the costs rose beyond her home equity loan. Those best-of-the-best picks, based more on the latest fashions than her needs, broke both her budget and her design.

PureWow.com, an entertainment digital media site, estimated whether the lifestyles of some popular TV characters were realistic.[47] Take Mindy Lahiri of the series *The Mindy Project*, living in New York City. PureWow rated the spacious, well-appointed apartment a 2 out of 10 for realism, stating that even Kim Kardashian's OB/GYN couldn't afford it. Mindy is well paid, but not well enough to be able to afford anything like the home portrayed on the show.

And what about those home improvement shows? Those beautiful remodels will cost you more than the program's producers spent. If you've ever had a kitchen or bathroom remodeled, you know what I'm talking about. Kiplinger.com reported that "advertisers provide free materials, and some contractors that appear on the shows are working at discounted rates for promotional reasons."[48] Yet the images that we see form our basis for how "normal" people live.

Comparisons to the people you know can mislead you too. Your coworkers, who should be making about what you're making, somehow manage to buy a new luxury car or live in a spacious modern home with all the fancy finishes. Unfortunately, you only see what they are spending, and you don't see what they are saving, which may be nothing.

Having a savings goal and working toward it can be an effective way to overcome your concern that you are not keeping up with your neighbors, coworkers, or whoever else you may be comparing your lifestyle to. Keeping track of your progress and comparing where you are to where you were is much more satisfying than comparing what you have to what they have.

Good Intentions, No Follow-Through

Alas, we are eternal optimists and therefore don't see the mistakes we are making. We are overly optimistic that we will take future actions that require self-control or work, like saving more and spending less or joining our company retirement plan.

Our optimism keeps us from seeing the downside of our behavior. In addition to not realizing that we are unlikely to do something that we put off to some future time, we tend to believe things will be the same in the future as they have been in the past. This can cause us to believe that we can always make more money because we've always made money before. Or we may believe that somehow things will work out in the end because they always have so far.

A friend told me that she was worried about her and her husband's financial future and she wanted to save more. But she was having a hard time getting him on board. She told me he thought he would always be able to make more money; therefore, saving more—or in other words, giving up more today—wasn't worth it. Of course, there are many things that could get in the way of earning an income in the future, but we fail to believe in the possibility of a bad outcome, so we don't dwell on it.

This at least partially explains why so many who are in their fifties still have little saved for their retirement. But you can improve your odds that you will do better. Studies show that making a concrete plan will increase the likelihood you will follow through.[49]

For example, if you've been meaning to join your company's retirement savings plan but haven't gotten around to it, put a date on your calendar to sign up. Include in your plan what you need to do, which might be to visit the human resources office or simply to visit the retirement plan's website. Tell someone about what you're going to do, maybe your spouse or a close friend. Telling someone helps cement the commitment in your brain.

Allocating a specific time, clearly identifying the things that need to be done, and voicing your intentions to someone else will all help you follow through on your good intentions.

No One Is Born to Save

Some people have an easier time taking the long view when it comes to saving and spending than others. But that doesn't mean saving comes naturally to anyone.

In a paper titled "Personality, Past Behaviour and Saving Intention: A Test of an Extended Model of the Theory of Planned Behaviour," researchers at the University of Padova in Italy identified a few personality traits that predicted whether a person was more likely to be a saver.[50] Using the Big Five profile, which measures personality on a sliding scale for five traits (openness to experience, conscientiousness, extraversion, agreeableness, and neuroticism), they tested whether personality influenced a person's intention to save. People who scored low on the extroversion scale (introverts) were more likely to be savers than people who scored high on the scale (extroverts). Scoring high on the conscientiousness scale also was associated with saving. Introverts tend to take time to act on their thoughts, while extroverts are quicker to make decisions. It could be that introverts naturally give themselves the time they need to put distance between themselves and temptation.

In a separate study titled "Psychological, Social and Economic Determinants of Saving: Comparing Recurrent and Total Savings," researchers at University College London found that savers tended to be people who believed they were in control of their own destiny, whereas non-savers were more likely to believe that external forces had a large influence on their lives.[51] Savers tended to be more structured, particularly in their approach to money management, whereas non-savers tended to be more flexible.

If you tend to be more deliberate in your actions, you may find it easier to learn to save, but anyone can do it. The more your natural tendencies make saving difficult for you, the more important it is for you to take advantage of services that make saving automatic. These include contributing to your company retirement savings plan or having a direct deposit from your pay to a savings account. Most banks will also do an automatic transfer from your main bank account to one that is harder to access. By taking the money out of reach, these services will help save you from yourself.

This Isn't Easy for Anyone

The very wealthy are not immune to difficulty in managing their financial lives. The list of highly paid celebrities who have filed for bankruptcy is long. Gary Busey, who has starred in dozens of films and had parts on several television shows, filed for bankruptcy in 2012. He had $50,000 to his name and owed more than $1 million in debts. MC Hammer filed for bankruptcy just six years after the release of an album that made $33 million. He had nearly $14 million in debts.[52] Allen Iverson, an eleven-time NBA All-Star, pulled in at least $154 million over his basketball career plus additional money from his music career, but at one point he told his wife he couldn't afford a cheeseburger.[53]

The Center for Retirement Research found that Americans across all income brackets have trouble making ends meet. Of households in the top one-third by income (adjusted for the number of people in the household), one in three report having difficulty covering regular expenses, and one in four would have a hard time coming up with $2,000. In the middle third by income, almost 60 percent report having difficulty covering expenses, and over a third would have a hard time coming up with $2,000.[54]

Even those who have the education and should know better can make mistakes. In a *Bloomberg News* article, economist Alicia Munnell outlined what she did and didn't do right in preparing for retirement. Despite having a PhD in economics from Harvard and working for the Federal Reserve, the US Treasury, the President's Council of Economic Advisers, and the Boston College Center for Retirement Research, Munnell didn't take a good hard look at how much she would need to have saved up if she were to maintain her standard of living in retirement until she was in her fifties. When she finally did take a hard look at her finances, she found a glaring gap between what she and her husband, an attorney, were spending and what they would be able to spend when they retired. After working with a financial planner to help close the gap, the Munnells sold their large home and downsized. While she and her husband are in good shape now, she voiced concern about the number of people who will not have enough money to live comfortably in retirement.[55]

We Can Learn to Save

Saving for retirement or other distant expenses is difficult. The amounts are large and may seem unattainable. With retirement, the variables to consider can be overwhelming. How long will you live? What will your income be in the future, and therefore how much do you need to replace? What kinds of investment returns can you expect? What will Social Security provide, if anything? There are ways to simplify how we think about these questions, but the one most Americans use is to not think about it at all.

Saving for the future, while complex and potentially unnatural, can be learned. But how are you to learn it? While many parents teach their kids a few general financial basics, most don't teach them about the more complex areas of credit and long-term saving. In a survey done by U.S. Bank, only about half of parents taught their kids about credit, and only a third talked to their kids about saving for retirement.[56]

An effective education program in personal finance could instill good financial habits in more people. It could result in fewer young people taking on too much debt, a better ability to finance education for their children, and greater financial security in retirement.

But personal finance is not taught in most public schools. Only seventeen states require high school students to receive any education in personal finance, and only five states require a stand-alone course in the subject.[57] Kids generally don't receive any instruction in how to manage a budget or the downside of debt, let alone the need to save for the future.

Employers do provide some education around their retirement plans. It is designed to explain the investment options in the plan and get people to make investment selections. Education events usually occur when there are changes in the provider for the plan or big changes in the investment options. If an employee isn't at the company when the event occurs, they are left to their own devices. And while the education helps, it doesn't provide a broader understanding of how to free up money so it's available to invest in the first place.

The result of the absence of a reliable way to learn about money is a lack of understanding of basic financial concepts. In three separate studies, one in 2009, one in 2012 and the last in 2015, the FINRA Investor Education Foundation found that Americans struggle to plan ahead and make optimal financial decisions. Only 31 percent of respondents to the 2015 National

Financial Capabilities Study had been exposed to financial education through school or work, and only 21 percent of those who had been offered an educational opportunity actually participated.[58] Participants in the 2015 study were asked five questions related to concepts of compound interest, inflation, mortgage terms, bond prices, and stock market risk. These concepts are fundamental to everyone's financial life, so it's not unreasonable to expect most people to get four or five out of five. Yet the average score was only 3.2 questions out of five. Only 14 percent of those surveyed were able to answer all five questions, and only 37 percent were able to answer four or more questions.[59]

The same study also found that 60 percent of Americans have not saved enough money to cover at least three months of expenses, and 41 percent engaged in expensive credit card habits like paying only the minimum payment, making late payments, and taking cash advances. Only 37 percent have tried to figure out how much money they will need in retirement.[60]

A little education did help. Those who had participated in personal finance educational opportunities did better when answering questions about basic financial concepts. And evidence from other social issues bears out the promise of education.

If young people were to receive some education in personal financial concepts while in primary and secondary school, it could help. It has made a difference in other critical areas. In the 1990s, the nation was faced with an HIV/AIDS epidemic. Sex education became more prevalent in schools. As a result, teen pregnancies and the incidence of unsafe sexual activities declined dramatically.[61] Numerous studies on smoking have shown that educating adolescents on its negative effects can reduce the number of teenagers who take it up.

Even very complex activities can be learned. Take driving, for example. You only have to teach a teenager to drive to understand that it's a miracle anyone can drive at all. First there is the physical operation of the car. You have to apply just the right amount of gas to go the speed that you intend. The intended speed will change frequently with the road you are traveling, the traffic, and unexpected obstacles. At the same time, you have to monitor your surroundings. You have to constantly be aware of what is in front of you, beside you, and behind you. On top of that, you have to signal your turns, search for road signs, and find a radio station that's actually playing music. Operating a car is incredibly complex, yet most of us do it without even thinking about it. You've probably experienced the phenomenon of arriving at your destination with no memory of what happened along the way. That is because you don't have to think about driving to be successful at it. It is a skill that you have learned and honed with practice.

In order to learn a new skill, it is best if we receive immediate and clear feedback and have lots of opportunities to practice.[62] When we learn to drive, we know immediately if we have done something wrong or right through the action or sound of the car (or the screams of nearby pedestrians). We also have the opportunity to practice.

When it comes to our financial lives, it doesn't seem like we have the same advantages. There are no immediate consequences if we don't have a rainy-day fund or don't fund our retirement account. If we run up our credit card debt, it is often easy to get additional credit, so aside from higher monthly payments, there aren't any immediate consequences to that either.

However, success in these bigger, longer-term savings objectives depends on what you do every day. You really do have many opportunities to practice. And there are rewards. Seeing your savings balances grow or your debt balances decline can be very gratifying. The tips already provided in this chapter will help you hone your saving skills as well as create better financial habits.

- Be mindful of your spending. Use cash where possible and track all your transactions.
- Use services like your company retirement savings plan, direct deposit, or automatic transfers to automatically take money out of contention and stash it away.
- Set spending and savings goals.
- Track your progress toward your goals frequently and celebrate your milestones.

If They Can Do It, We Can Do It

The savings track record of people in other countries supports the idea that it is possible to learn to save. In China, the average household savings rate is around 30 percent.[63] The average household savings rate in Germany is just under 10 percent. Our own in the United States is less than 5 percent.[64]

Whether a savings rate is reasonable depends largely on what other sources of income a person will have when they stop working. China has invested in improving health care and expanding its pension system, but these are new developments. The average Chinese citizen doesn't expect that the government will provide any safety net at all. So people save for potential medical bills and the prospect of losing their jobs as well as for their own retirements and their children's education.

Contrast that with Germany, where the average person receives about 70 percent of their preretirement income in a government-provided pension and where there is government support for the unemployed and a government-sponsored health care system.[65] The 10 percent savings rate looks logical for Germany.

Here in the United States, our savings rate also averaged about 10 percent up until the 1990s.[66] Social Security replaced about 43 percent of the average worker's income at the full retirement age, and for many, traditional defined benefit pension plans covered another good chunk.[67] However, in the 1990s the savings rate dropped to under 7 percent and fell further with the new millennium. The average savings rate since 2000 has been below 5 percent.

The fact that our savings rate is lower now than it was in the 1980s doesn't make any sense. Pension plans began their steady decline in the 1990s to the point now where they are almost nonexistent in the private sector. Looking ahead, Social Security is expected to replace a smaller percentage of preretirement income unless significant reform can increase funding for the program. With few people receiving a guaranteed pension income from their employer and the prospect of lower Social Security benefits as a percentage of preretirement income, why are we saving less than ever?

It may be that as a country we simply haven't adapted to the reality that we need to save for our own financial futures. According to a Pew Research study, the early baby boomers (born between 1946 and 1955), who began reaching the traditional retirement age in 2011, will be able to replace 70 to 80 percent of their preretirement incomes. Many are still retiring with some pension benefits. They had little need to acquire the skills to manage the complexities of saving enough to live on for decades after they stopped working.

It is the late boomers (born 1956 to 1965) and Generation X (born 1966 to 1975), who will begin reaching the traditional retirement age in 2021 and 2031, respectively, who will most feel the pinch of the dramatic shift in our system of retirement benefits. Late boomers are expected to only be able to replace

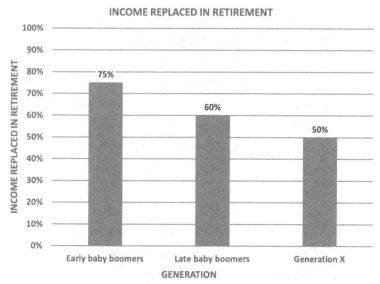

Source: Gist and Hatch., *Retirement Security Across Generations.*

60 percent of their preretirement income, and Generation X will only be able to replace half.

This will mean a substantial shift down in their standards of living. As these people begin to struggle for financial security and our economy is impacted by a substantial decline in spending for nearly 20 percent of our population, we may begin to see the average savings rates rise.[68] The need for education in personal financial management will become more apparent and, like sex education, may find a home in schools.

Certainly the government has already taken notice of the pending problem. Policy changes, such as the Pension Protection Act of 2006, which encouraged companies to implement automatic enrollment in their retirement plans as well as automatic increases of employee contribution rates, will help improve the situation. There are efforts at all levels of government to increase worker access to retirement savings accounts through their employers.

However, these efforts alone will not fill the gap. Individuals must learn to manage their personal finances more effectively, and we need to return to a culture where saving is valued above spending.

Main Ideas

1. Saving money is not natural for human beings. There are many natural tendencies that stand in the way.
2. Saving for long-term large goals, like retirement, is a skill that, while complex, can be learned. Success lies in what you do every day.
3. Unlike driving, there isn't a consistent process for learning to save. Parents, schools, and employers have all fallen short in providing a foundational understanding of personal financial concepts.
4. You can overcome your natural instincts and build good financial habits by being mindful about how you spend your money, setting spending and savings goals, and tracking your progress toward those goals frequently.
5. The most effective way to save money is to make it automatic. Have savings automatically deducted from your pay through your company retirement plan, direct deposited to your savings account, and/or automatically transferred from your main account to a savings account that is less accessible.

Chapter 3

Everyone Needs to Save

YOUR FUTURE FINANCIAL SECURITY IS AN OBLIGATION, LIKE your rent, utilities, and debt payments. But no one sends you a statement so you can pay the correct amount. You have to save on your own. It's time you start treating your financial security like the bill that it is.

Everyone needs to save. You need to save money to support yourself when you stop working for pay. You will need to set aside money for the unexpected, such as a job loss or prolonged health issue. Avoiding debt wherever possible will reduce the costs of what you buy and ensure your financial security. If you have kids, providing for their educations will make a world of difference in their future financial security.

Yes, it may be that your current expenses preclude you from saving; however, a hard look at those expenses will likely turn up some areas that can be cut back. The usual stories you may be telling yourself need a good hard look too. Here are some of the excuses I've heard.

I Will Work Until I Die

I hear this story a lot. Sam, who just turned sixty, owns his own business, and that is his plan. He was divorced when his son was young, and alimony and child support payments put a big dent in his income. These ended a few years ago, when his son turned eighteen.

He had planned to set more savings aside with that extra money but soon began to experience health issues. Being self-employed, his out-of-pocket health care costs are high. With no savings to speak of, Sam will simply work until he can't any longer. His current lifestyle far exceeds what Social Security will cover, even if he waits to collect it until age seventy, when benefits will be at their maximum. It is highly likely that there will be a gap of time between when Sam can't work any longer and when he dies that could be quite long. His work is physically grueling. Sam is on his feet all day. He often has to be in uncomfortable positions for prolonged periods, and there is a great deal of repetitive motion that wears on his muscles and joints.

Sam could have made different lifestyle choices, even when his son was young, that would have reduced his cost of living and freed up income for saving. There were less expensive housing options, for example. But he enjoys his lifestyle and doesn't believe giving it up is the answer.

The problem—creating his own retirement plan—seems insurmountable, so he is making the most out of today. He has almost fatalistically refused to look at his future. At this stage, he will not be able to avoid a big change in the way he lives if he is forced to give up his work.

According to the Employee Benefit Research Institute (EBRI) 2015 Retirement Confidence Survey, more than a third of today's workers plan to retire after the age of sixty-five, up from a quarter in the 2005 survey. More than one in four in that group plans to work to age seventy or later, and one in ten plans on never retiring.

But this annual survey has consistently found that half of retirees retire sooner than planned, citing a variety of issues, including health problems and corporate downsizing.[69] Sam doesn't have to worry about downsizing, but his health problems may prove to be an issue. Even if you love your work, it isn't realistic to think that you will always be able to do it. You need to set money aside if you want to live comfortably when you do stop working.

I Can Always Make More Money

Another story that is related to "I will work forever" is "I can always make more money." The difference here is the implied plan to put money aside for the future—in the future. This mind-set seems to be common among people who have high incomes. It often doesn't work out well because, as we already know, we aren't any more likely to do something tomorrow if we haven't done it today.

A portfolio manager I know told me the story of a doctor in a group of orthopedists. This doctor lived very well, with a spacious home atop a hill overlooking his community. The national average annual income for orthopedic surgeons is $421,000. Yet this particular surgeon had only managed to sock away $400,000, less than a year of his likely income, for his retirement. Based on what he had saved, it probably wouldn't pay for his lifestyle for more than a couple of years. When his firm eased him out of his practice at the age of sixty-two, he was far from prepared.

This is not an unusual story with doctors. A report by Medscape.com indicated that about 23 percent of doctors aged fifty, and about 12 percent of those aged sixty, had a **net worth** of less than $500,000.[70] Your net worth is the difference between the value of your assets and the total amount of debt you hold.

In their book *The Millionaire Next Door*, Thomas J. Stanley and William D. Danko called people like these doctors UAWs: Under

Accumulators of Wealth. The authors found that high-income producers who are UAWs work to spend.[71] They may be trapped by the image of how and where someone in their line of work is supposed to live. There is pressure to decorate the house and drive a car similar to everyone else's in the neighborhood. Their vacations must stack up to their colleagues', and of course their kids have to attend similarly prestigious schools. They are unaware that their colleagues may be equally strapped. It can't go on forever.

The following chart shows the percentage of your income that you would need to save for a reasonable shot at financial security at different ages.

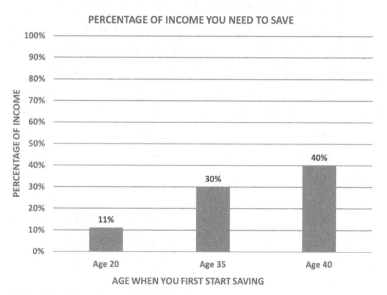

Source: Kadlec, "What Savings Rate You Need"

It won't always be possible to earn more money or to save later. At some point, it won't be possible to earn enough to make up for lost time. If you think it's hard to save 11 percent of your pay in your twenties, how hard will it be to save 40 percent in your forties?

I Don't Have a Retirement Plan through Work

It would seem like not having a retirement plan through work would be a great incentive to set money aside, since there is no other backstop. But that is not the case.

Those who do not have a work-related retirement plan are far less likely to have retirement savings than those who do. Of those without a work-related retirement plan, only 10 percent have more than $25,000 saved for their future.[72] This disparity in savings has become a concern for governments. Some states are even working on creating state-sponsored 401(k) plans for workers who otherwise wouldn't have access to one through work.

In the absence of an employer-sponsored retirement plan, the options are wide open; therefore, it may be hard to figure out how and what to save on your own. You may be simply unaware of what is available, and if you are aware, you might be overwhelmed by the array of options. There are a variety of tax-advantaged accounts available, from traditional and Roth individual retirement accounts (IRAs) to accounts specifically designed for the self-employed and small businesses. These are all described in chapter 9. But even if tax-advantaged accounts didn't exist, you could still save.

I Will Inherit Money

Maybe your parents have money. Not many people in America get an inheritance. Around 21 percent of Americans receive money from the older generations in their families, and most of the money transferred belongs to the very wealthy.[73] About 15 percent of baby boomers (born between 1946 and 1964) and 21 percent of those born after 1964 expect to receive an inheritance. Even if you are among this cohort, don't count on an inheritance to bail you out. The median amount inherited is only around $49,000.[74]

More people are living longer than ever before, and those extra years chew up cash. Whatever savings your parents have will likely be mostly spent over their lifetimes. According to the Social Security Administration, an individual who is currently seventy years old has a good chance of living to be eighty-four or older.[75] That is a long time to spread out your retirement savings. And retirees are finding life more expensive.

More retirees are holding debt than they did even a decade ago, which increases their monthly cost of living. Almost two-thirds of people between the ages of sixty-five and seventy-five and nearly four in ten of those older than seventy-five have debt, mostly in the form of a mortgage on their home. Between 2001 and 2011, the amount of mortgage debt held by those over the age of sixty-five increased from $43,400 to $79,000. As a result, their monthly housing costs were about three times that of seniors without housing debt.[76]

Health care is another rising cost. Just because your parents are eligible for Medicare doesn't mean they don't pay for health care. The average out-of-pocket costs for those aged sixty-five to seventy-five, including premiums, is over $4,000 per person per year, and it only goes higher with age. For those aged seventy-five to eighty-five, the annual expenses rise to over $5,200, and for those over the age of eighty-five, the annual expenses go up to $8,200.[77] You may wind up helping your parents out financially rather than getting an inheritance from them.

My House Is My Retirement Plan

What about your house? Are you planning to sell your home, downsize, and rescue your financial security that way? For most Americans, the value of their home represents two-thirds of their net worth.[78]

You do have to live somewhere. Even if you downsize, the net proceeds from your old house are not likely to go far after you buy your new, smaller house. Remember those smaller houses are going up in value just like yours, and there will be expenses associated with selling your house and moving.

To get the most out of the trade, you may need to move to a lower-cost area. Moving could mean you are moving away from your friends and family. On the other hand, if you are mortgage-free or at least have a high level of equity in your home relative to your mortgage, you may be able to tap that equity to help make ends meet.

One way to lower your cost of living is to move in with your kids. This strategy actually worked out well for Hayden and Sophia. Along with Hayden's parents, they sold their 1950s bungalows in San Jose, California, where even during the real estate downturn housing prices were astronomical. They pooled their proceeds to buy a larger home with a mother-in-law suite. This allowed Hayden to be within earshot of his aging parents and allowed them all to afford a lifestyle they couldn't on their own. As long as you plan this with your kids, it can be a great solution; however, no one wants to wind up in this situation by accident.

I Have a Pension

What if you have a pension? If you do, you are rare and lucky. If you work for a government entity, belong to a union, or work for one of the few remaining large companies who offer a traditional defined benefit pension plan, congratulations. A traditional defined benefit pension plan guarantees you a monthly income when you retire based on your years of service and your salary during your final years of work. You will still need to save, but not as much as those without these benefits. Your employer is doing some of the saving for you.

If you have a traditional pension plan, why would you need to save? Pension benefits are increasingly being reduced as employers try to contain costs, so your pension may not be what you expect. There is also risk to your benefits, because some pensions are underfunded.

Even if these problems are not the case at your employer, most defined benefit pension plans are designed to be one leg of a three-legged stool. The pension provides for some of your living expenses, but it is expected that Social Security and your own personal savings will provide the rest.

An EBRI study found that, for the top half of wage earners, defined benefit pension plans do not replace enough of a participant's income to support their same lifestyle in retirement. Even those whose income is just below the median may have a hard time living on only the pension benefits and Social Security with no additional savings.[79] And federal government and some state government employees may not be eligible for Social Security.

It's Never Too Late

Even if you haven't been a big saver in the past, there's no time like the present to start. Of course, the earlier you start, the easier it is, but later in life you have fewer obligations to get in your way. As the Chinese proverb goes, "A journey of a thousand miles begins with one step."

What if you can't save enough to replace your current income? T. Rowe Price did a survey of recent retirees who had at least some money in a 401(k) account or IRA and found that most are able to manage. On average, the more than 1,000 retirees surveyed live on about two-thirds of their preretirement income. While many were surprised by how hard it is to live without their

Gene

At sixty-one, Gene was tired of working. He had a long commute, and he found his role as a project manager exhausting. There were things that he wanted to do while he was healthy, like spend more time skiing or motorcycling. But retirement was still several years away.

Gene was always the primary income earner in the family. His wife, Roberta, worked for a bit of extra spending money, but Gene's income covered the bulk of the expenses for their family of four. He had saved in his company 401(k) plan off and on, but between job changes and life's expenses, the balance wasn't big to begin with.

Gene's retirement savings was the family's only savings, so when it came time for the kids to head to college, he tapped it to pay for their education. Unfortunately, the timing was bad, and the balance was at a low point due to turmoil in the stock markets. As a result, he had a hole to fill.

Gene made a plan. He took a good hard look at his expenses to understand what kind of income he and his wife needed to live comfortably. Then he did a little research to understand what would be coming his way from Social Security at the different filing ages, and he made some decisions.

First, while he was tired of working, he planned to work until he was seventy so he could maximize his Social Security benefit. He and Roberta would have a lot more spending money if they didn't have a mortgage. That meant they would need to sell their San Francisco

Bay Area home when he did stop working and move to a cheaper location. He expected the equity he'd have by that time would allow him to live debt-free.

Finally, he kept his spending low so he could maximize his savings. He saved over 40 percent of his annual income. Having a strategy is at least half of the battle, and just knowing what to expect made a difference for Gene and Roberta.

working income, 85 percent said they didn't need to spend as much as they did while they were working to be happy.[80]

Whatever you save will make life easier when you can no longer work. The advantage of saving as much as possible as early as possible is that you have more choices. But that doesn't mean if you're late you will have no choices. Figure out where you are, and from there you can discover where you can go with what you have.

Retirement Isn't the Only Thing

Setting money aside in your company's (or your personal) retirement plan isn't enough. Once the money is set aside in these accounts, it's hard to get at and could cost you more than just what you need in the moment. Depending on the account, you could have to pay taxes and early withdrawal penalties.

For true financial security, you need to save for emergencies and you need to avoid debt. That means that you should be setting aside money for the chance that you lose a job, for expenses that you know will come up but don't know when, and for big-ticket items like furniture or vacations. If you want to help your kids out, you will also want to save for their college education.

Emergencies

Your first priority is to have money for an emergency. It is even more important than saving for retirement.

Terry is a massage therapist. While bicycle commuting to his office, he was hit by a car. Fortunately, his injuries weren't serious, but he did break his collarbone and several ribs. He couldn't do any massages after the accident. He had no income while he recovered. Stuff happens, and you need to be financially prepared to weather the storm.

A common piece of advice suggests that you should have at least three months of living expenses in emergency savings. Three months might not cut it, but it's a good place to start. One way to gauge how much you really need would be to consider how long it will take you to find a new job if you lose the one you have. To avoid having your financial future derailed—or at the very least set back—setting money aside that's not part of your retirement plan will create an important buffer. You will find a worksheet to calculate what you need for emergencies in chapter 8.

So that you don't go into debt for unexpected expenses, you also need to make as few of them unexpected as possible. What previously may have been an emergency doesn't have to be. You can look ahead for expenses that you can predict will come up even if you don't know when they will come up. If you have a car or home, you will have maintenance expenses. These will be easier to deal with if you've set something aside each month toward them. Similarly, if your health insurance has a deductible or you pay out of pocket for prescriptions or doctor's visits, you will need to set some money aside each month for these even if you aren't currently sick.

The Big Stuff

You can also avoid going into debt for your big-ticket purchases if you save ahead. Say you put your $2,000 sectional sofa on your credit card and take a year to pay it off. Credit card interest rates average over 15 percent, so your sofa will actually cost you $2,166 if you make equal payments over the course of the year.

Buying a car? The typical interest rates are lower than credit cards, just under 4.0 percent in 2017, but a five-year loan on a $20,000 car will cost you an extra $1,600.[81] If you are buying a house, saving a down payment of 20 percent will allow you to avoid paying private mortgage insurance and lower your payment. With any big purchase you make, setting money aside beforehand will cost you less.

An even bigger advantage when you avoid buying things with debt is the financial flexibility that you will keep. You can't choose to not make a payment on your outstanding debt. As your debt grows, the payments will crowd out other uses for your money.

Before long, it may be hard to pay for other parts of your life. These debt payments also put you at greater risk of a financial catastrophe if you lose your job or can't work due to an injury or illness. The money you must come up with every month to just get by will be larger than it would be without the debt.

College

Another big-ticket item that will cost less if you save ahead is your children's college education. The average cost to attend in-state public universities, including tuition, fees, and room and board, was nearly $20,000 per year for the 2015–2016 school year. The cost of private school was more than double that.[82]

Seven in ten graduating college seniors in 2014 had student debt, with an average balance of nearly $30,000.[83] The monthly payment on loans of that magnitude is over $300 when using the standard repayment plan.[84] For young people just starting out on their own, that is a big burden. It limits their financial flexibility and can delay their ability to save for their future.

If you are saving enough for yourself, there is no greater gift you can give to your kids than providing them with a college education that is debt-free. However, only about half of parents of college-bound students do save for college, and of those who do, on average they had saved only $10,000 in 2015.[85]

Scott and Beth had some money saved for their two kids' college educations but not enough to cover the full cost. They also had retirement savings but were a little behind if they wanted to leave their jobs at a traditional retirement age. Their big decision, as their daughter entered college, was whether to fill the gap in educational expenses or have the kids take out loans.

Filling the gap would require them to drastically reduce their retirement savings while the kids were in school and as a result set back the time when they would be able to leave work while maintaining their lifestyle. Families need to make these decisions together, and there is no right or wrong answer. Understanding the trade-offs is the real key.

While graduating with student loan debt is not ideal, your kids have more options and more time to dig themselves out of their holes than you do. They may be able to work before college to raise some money toward education expenses, and they can work part-time while in school as well. Their college choices can also reduce their costs and limit the need for loans. For example, going to a public community college for the first two years can reduce the cost of tuition and fees by almost two-thirds relative to the same expenses at a public four-year school, and living at home (with you) can reduce the total costs of a four-year education by as much as $40,000.[86]

You, on the other hand, have fewer options. If you are not currently saving for your own financial security, that needs to be your priority. Just as you are told in the airline safety briefing before every flight, save yourself first. The longer you delay, the more difficult it will be. If you do not have an emergency fund and are not making progress on your retirement savings, put paying for college on the back burner.

For most, there is no good excuse for not saving. Aside from saving for retirement, you also need money for emergencies and other expenses that are part of everyday living but don't come with a monthly bill. If you aren't saving, you are living beyond your means.

Who Really Can't Afford to Save

There are some households that really can't make ends meet. The median household income in the United States at the end of 2014 was $53,657.[87] In the ten largest states by population, this is just about enough to get by if you have two kids and either you or your spouse works, but not both of you. It is not nearly enough if you have two kids and both you and your spouse work, nor is it enough if you are a single parent of two kids, primarily because of the cost of childcare.

The following chart shows the living wage required to make basic ends meet in the ten largest states, according to the Living Wage Calculator created and maintained by the Massachusetts Institute of Technology.[88] The Living Wage Calculator was designed to capture the basic subsistence income required for a person or family given geographic differences in the cost of living. The model considers the cost of food, childcare, health insurance, housing, transportation,

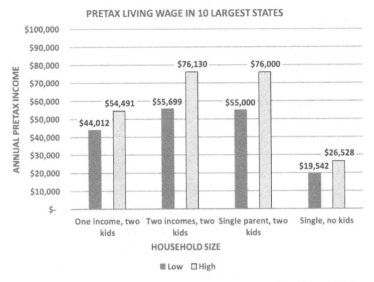

PRETAX LIVING WAGE IN 10 LARGEST STATES

Source: Dr. Amy K. Glasmeier and MIT, Living Wage Calculator, http://livingwage.mit.edu/

and other basic necessities. But it does not cover any luxuries like eating out, entertainment, or vacations, and it certainly does not allow for any savings.

While the median single-person household and the median married household nationwide generally do earn enough to get by comfortably and set aside savings, about a third of households with four people make less than the living wage.[89] Families living near the living wage are on the edge of financial disaster. A job loss or short hospitalization is all it takes to knock them off their feet. Because they cannot save, they have a difficult time changing their circumstances and become trapped in a constant struggle to remain afloat.

Fortunately, this is not most of us. Most of us do have enough income to save at least some money. Even small amounts can make a huge difference in your future financial security.

Vocabulary

Net worth: The value of all your assets (home, retirement accounts, savings, etc.) minus the value of the debt you owe (mortgage, credit cards, student loans, etc.).

Main Ideas

1. Everyone needs to save money.
2. It is never too late to start saving.
3. Beyond saving for retirement, you will need to save for emergencies and other expenses to avoid going into debt.
4. Debt reduces your financial flexibility and security.
5. Paying for your children's college education is a true gift, but if you aren't saving enough for yourself, saving for college needs to be on the back burner.

PART 2

Chapter 4

You Can Save If You Have a Goal

THE KEY TO SUCCESS IN ANY ENDEAVOR IS TO HAVE A GOAL. Whether you have a grand goal, like running a marathon, or a more mainstream goal, like getting fit, the first thing you must do is decide what you're going for. Saving is no different. You must have a goal and commit to it.

Goals help you define what you will and what you won't do. They highlight your trade-offs so you know what you are gaining and giving up with each choice. If you want to get fit, maybe you will get up early every morning to work out. You won't sleep in even if you don't feel like working out. You will feel good about the choice because it moves you closer to your goal. As you start to see results, your resolve will grow.

The same is true of savings goals. Prioritizing saving over spending won't seem like a sacrifice if you are committed to it. It seems rewarding instead. As your savings grow, you are getting closer to achieving your goal. Having a goal can produce dramatic results. The following stories may help you begin to formulate your own.

FIREd Up

There is a movement that you may have heard about: the Financial Independence, Retire Early, or FIRE, movement. It's made up of people who are leaving the workforce at surprisingly young ages. To achieve that goal, they live very differently than most.

While they have good incomes, the key to their success is in how little they spend. To be able to retire very early, they generally spend less than half their income and therefore save more than half.

FIREs can spend so little because they make deliberate choices about how they live. They live close enough to work to not need to own a car, for example, or if they do own a car, it's a modest one. They keep their housing costs low relative to their incomes, and they find low-cost ways to enjoy life, like camping on vacation or eating home-cooked meals. These choices may seem like a sacrifice to some of you, but to the FIRE crowd, these are easy choices that help them achieve their goals.

Take Justin McCurry. Justin worked in engineering, and his wife worked in accounting and finance. Justin retired at the age of thirty-three in 2013 with just under $1.3 million in savings and investments. His wife continued to work for a few years then left her job in 2016.

Justin and his wife are lifelong savers. Their family of five was able to save half of their income for the ten years he worked after college. They made good money as professionals. Their combined income peaked at around $150,000, but their contributions to savings averaged $77,000 annually over the ten years.

Justin decided early on that he didn't want to work into his sixties or beyond, and he chose a lifestyle that would accommodate that goal. The McCurrys live in a modest home, drive modest cars, and eat at home for the most part. They take fantastic vacations and plan to send their children to college. They are currently living on about $32,000 per year.[90] Justin blogs about his experience and offers advice at www.rootofgood.com.

You don't have to start out as a lifelong saver though. Jeremy and Winnie Jacobson both grew up in lower-income households and put themselves through college with student loans. Jeremy had $40,000 worth of debt when he graduated. After working for sixteen years, they left corporate life to travel the world in 2012. They live mostly on their investment income.

How were they able to leave the corporate life so soon? They spent their first five or so years getting out of debt. Then they spent ten years saving like crazy. They lived in a comfortable 900-square-foot apartment in a walkable neighborhood of Seattle, so they didn't own a car. To get around, they walked, biked, or took public transportation. They ate most of their meals from their own kitchen and took advantage of free entertainment. The result was they were able to save an average of 70 percent of their income.

The Jacobsons live on about $4,000 per month now and have visited forty countries to date. They don't live like backpackers. In fact, they have been able to rent wonderful places, eat in restaurants, and enjoy the adventures offered wherever they have landed. Jeremy also blogs about his experience and offers advice at his website, www.gocurrycracker.com.[91]

Single Income, Five Kids

Though not part of the FIRE movement, the Economides did what many may think is impossible. They raised five children, bought and paid off two homes, helped their children graduate from college debt-free, took many wonderful family vacations, and saved for retirement all on a single income. In the first ten years of their marriage, while they paid off their first home, their average annual income was only $35,000. In today's dollars, that would be about $60,000 per year. Steve Economides was a graphic designer, and his wife, Annette, was a stay-at-home mom.[92]

The Economides are wizards of planning, and they squeeze every ounce of value out of whatever they buy. To raise a family of seven on one income, every dollar had to count. They planned every meal in advance so they avoided food waste. They had a master plan for how to clothe their kids so they could reuse what was in good shape after the older kids outgrew their clothes.

Nothing was left to impulse, chance, or serendipity. Early on, they embraced a debt-free lifestyle, only borrowing to buy their homes. The mortgages were paid off as quickly as possible. While their income grew, they continued to live frugally and build their savings. They now offer advice through their website and newsletters at www.moneysmartfamily.com, and they have written a best-selling book, *America's Cheapest Family Gets You Right on the Money*.

Jeff and Me

My husband, Jeff, and I didn't have big hairy goals like the McCurrys and Jacobsons, and as a two-professional household, we had more disposable income than the Economides. Jeff and I were able to reach financial independence about a dozen years before the traditional retirement age, which seems less impressive after reading these other families' stories. Yet it is still unusual among people in our age and income brackets.

Jeff never wanted to work beyond the age of fifty-five, so we prioritized saving for retirement. We paid off the little nonmortgage debt we had as quickly as possible. Then we set about paying off our mortgage, all the while making sure we were meeting our savings targets.

We were lucky. Our dual income was in the upper end of the income brackets. I also worked for my company long enough to be eligible for a small pension that will help stretch our savings even further when it begins paying benefits. These are advantages that many don't have, but they are not what drove our success. My colleagues at work were in similar income brackets and had similar benefits, but they don't have the same financial freedom.

The secret to our success is that Jeff and I saved first. Before we spent any money, we met our monthly savings goal. That defined our lifestyle and ensured that we were paying the bill for our financial freedom up front. We paid far less for our home than the amount of mortgage for which we could have qualified. We eat most of our meals at home, and while we've had some great vacations, their costs were well contained. These kinds of choices put us ahead of the game. Our house is paid off, and we are debt-free. We have money set aside for our daughter's college education as well as enough money to maintain our lifestyle for the rest of our lives.

What are the common threads here? We all had a goal. The McCurrys and the Jacobsons wanted out of the rat race as soon as possible. The Economides wanted to make ends meet on a single modest income, and Jeff and I wanted to have the freedom to leave the workforce in our fifties.

Your goals are likely different than mine or the other families mentioned here. You certainly do not need to have dramatic goals like retiring in your thirties or traveling the world. Your goals could be as simple as not having to work past a normal retirement age.

However, the following are goals that should be on everyone's list. You will find more information on these in the following chapters.

Goals	Tools/Strategies
Protect against financial setbacks	Have an emergency fund, eliminate nonmortgage debt, have disability and property insurance (chapter 8)
Retire by age _____	Contribute to employer retirement plan, individual retirement accounts, and additional savings as needed; eliminate all debt (chapters 7 and 9)
Take care of family if I die or cannot speak for myself	Will, life insurance, family trust, beneficiary designations, medical and financial powers of attorney, health care directive/living will (chapter 12)

Whatever your goals, the first step toward achieving them is to define them. In the immortal words of Yogi Berra, "You've got to be very careful if you don't know where you're going, because you might not get there."[93]

SMART

To be effective, goals need to be specific, measurable, attainable, realistic, and have a time frame. The SMART goal framework is broadly used for setting goals around anything from corporate projects to individual weight loss. SMART goals give you a clear vision of what you want to accomplish, let you focus on what is important to you, and motivate you.

Savings goals are no different from other goals, but you do need to be careful about the goal you are setting. Your goal should be about the thing you are saving for and not simply a money target. While money is an important part of your savings goal—the measurement part—by itself it is meaningless and uninspiring. It is what you will do with your money that will motivate you.

Many financial experts encourage you to define your goals in detail so you can more accurately plan for them. In his book *The Number*, Lee Eisenberg highlights the difficulty in setting detailed retirement goals. He raises questions about how you will live when you stop working for pay that frankly just can't be fully answered at the time when you need to begin saving. Questions like how healthy you will be, how and where you want to spend your retirement, and what would make you feel happy and fulfilled are important.[94]

However, if you wait until you know the answers to these questions to develop a goal, none of the answers will matter. You will have few choices remaining. But you can define initial goals and then make changes along the way as you know more. For the time being, you could simply decide that you want to stop working at the normal retirement age and maintain your lifestyle. This simple goal is a SMART goal.

It is specific because it says exactly what you want to do—stop working at the normal retirement age. It is measurable because it says how you want to live. You want to live as you are living today, and your lifestyle can be defined by the amount of money you spend, making it measurable. Your retirement age is a specific time frame. Whether this goal is attainable and realistic does depend on when you start, but wherever you do start, you can set a goal that is realistic and attainable.

Living as you do today when you stop working at your normal retirement age is a long-term goal. To make that goal manageable, you will need to break it up into short- and medium-term goals. Short-term goals are how much you will save each month. Medium-term goals are how much you will save in a year, have saved in five years, and so on. Your medium-term goals may need to include gradual increases in your monthly savings over time.

As you go along, you will learn more. Maybe after your grand-kids arrive, you'll decide you want to live near them. Perhaps along the way you will develop a passion for a hobby where you'll want to spend more time. Health issues might come up. You can adjust your short- and medium-term goals to accommodate these refinements to your long-term goal.

And of course, retirement isn't your only goal. All your savings and other goals can be approached in this way.

If you set SMART goals, you will be able to easily visualize what you are shooting for, and your goals will become your pri-ority. That will make it easier for you to say no to things that are not your priority or would otherwise prevent you from achiev-ing your biggest goals. Breaking down big long-term goals into smaller short- and medium-term goals will make getting where you want to go more manageable and less overwhelming.

Specifically, How Much

How much will you need to have saved up before you can afford your same lifestyle in the future? About twenty-five times what you're spending minus income from other sources beyond your own savings—that is, if you are planning to stop working at the usual retirement age. This estimate is based on the 4 percent rule developed by financial planner William Bengen.

In 1994, Bengen studied thirty-year time periods beginning in 1926 to determine whether there was a withdrawal rate that a retiree could take and reasonably expect their money would last for at least thirty years. His conclusion was that a withdrawal rate starting at 4.5 percent of savings and increasing by the rate of inflation for all following years worked. Somehow the 0.5 percent was lost in the translation, and now his conclusion is commonly known as the 4 percent rule. In a 2012 *Financial Advisor* article, he revisited the study and found that this withdrawal rate remains reasonable.[95]

The withdrawal rate is how much you take out of savings. How much you take out of savings is what you spend minus any other sources of income you may have. You can calculate how much you spend in a year and therefore how much you need.

Look at your last paycheck. You are looking for your net income after all deductions for taxes and retirement savings. Once you have that number, subtract any additional money that you saved beyond deposits to your company retirement plan. The difference in these two numbers is how much you spent.

How do I know? If you didn't pay it out in taxes and you didn't save it, you must have spent it. The reason you don't simply take your net pay is because the cost of your benefits, like health and life insurance, are spending. You wouldn't want to miss those expenses.

Multiply your spending by the number of pay periods you have in a month, and you'll have your monthly spending. Here is a worksheet you can use.

	Example	*You*
Gross pay	$4,100	
Federal income tax	$563	
State income tax	$292	
Local payroll tax	$0	
Social Security	$243	

	Example	*You*
Medicare	$56	
401(k) contribution	$410	
Any other savings direct deposit	$0	
Pay after savings and taxes	**$2,536**	
Other savings	$0	
Spending	**$2,536**	
× pay periods per month	2	
Monthly spending	**$5,072**	

Now this might not take into account all your spending. For example, if you usually get a tax refund and you spend it rather than save it, you can add that to your spending. If you get a bonus that isn't reflected in your most recent pay and spend that instead of saving it, add that as well.

You may be surprised by how much you spend. Many are. It is hard to estimate your spending any other way besides this one or, alternatively, tracking each and every expense. Most people I talk to are surprised by how much they do spend, and their estimates, using what seem like reasonable assumptions for everyday expenses, run about 40 percent short.

Once you know what you spend, you can start figuring out what you will need to save in order to replace it when you stop working for pay. You won't have to pay for all of your lifestyle yourself. You will receive some benefits from Social Security, and if you work for the government, a union, or one of the small number of companies still offering pension benefits, you may receive a pension income.

You can get a projection of your Social Security benefits from the Social Security Administration at www.SSA.gov. There you will find calculators for a quick-and-dirty benefit estimate, or you can create an account and get what the administration is projecting specifically for you. You can get an estimate of pension benefits from your human resources department.

You will need to pay federal and state income taxes on your taxable income, so it's a good idea to include a provision for that. In the following example, a guess of 16 percent total for federal and state taxes based on the spending projected and current tax rates is used.

Subtract the estimate of Social Security benefits and any other income you might be expecting when you leave your job from the total spending including taxes. The result is what you will have to come up with on your own.

Source	Example	*You*
Spending	$5,072	
× future income tax rate guestimate (16%)	0.16	
= Taxes	$812	
Spending + taxes (what you need each month)	$5,884	
– Monthly Social Security benefit	$2,551	

Source	Example	*You*
– Monthly pension benefit	$0	
= Monthly savings withdrawal	$3,333	
Monthly withdrawal × 12 = annual withdrawal	$39,996	

As you can see in the example, you'll have a lot of ground to make up after Social Security, and the example shows one of the highest possible benefits. Without savings, most people will find Social Security far too little to live on, and that assumes the current promised payout rates. The chart on the next page shows how little income can be replaced by Social Security.[96]

If you take the annual savings withdrawal in the previous worksheet ($39,996) and multiply it by 25 (from the 4 percent rule), you get $999,900. It is a very big number.

If the number scares you and you don't believe you will need quite so much to live on in the future, you can back into your required total savings from the opposite direction. The same rule delivers a monthly income of $333 per $100,000 of savings. Four percent of $100,000 is $4,000. Divide that by 12, and you get $333 per month.

There are legitimate things that you can take out of your expenses. For example, if you will pay off your mortgage before you stop working, that is an expense you won't have in the future. If you are currently paying for college, either yours or your kids, you may not have that expense either.

But before you start shaving away at your future expenses, consider a couple of things. Health care expenses may take up

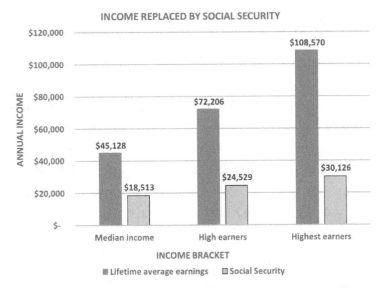

INCOME REPLACED BY SOCIAL SECURITY

Source: Clingman, Burkhalter, and Chaplain, "Replacement Rates for Hypothetical Retired Workers"

more of your spending in the future than they do today, and you may find new interests that take the place of the mortgage and other expenses you're planning to not have. So you may not spend less after all.

The one thing that you won't have to do once you stop working for pay is save money. The good news is, the more you save the less you spend, so the cost of replacing your lifestyle in the future will be lower.

The dollars involved in funding your lifestyle are large regardless of your current spending level. It may be hard to get your arms around having to save so much. Instead, per-paycheck and annual savings goals will be easier to work toward. Your company's retirement plan website likely has a calculator to help you, and if not, there are many calculators available for free online. The following list has just a few.

- CalcXML.com: Retirement Calculator
- Dinkytown.net: Calculators/Retirement Savings and Planning
- FinancialMentor.com: Calculators/Retirement Calculator

The three primary pieces of information used in retirement calculators are time, the rate of return, and the cost of the lifestyle you are trying to replace. The more time you have, the less you will need to save. The higher the rate of return you assume, the less you will need to save. But be careful that your assumed rate isn't unrealistic. Using a high rate of return that doesn't materialize will only cause you to need to save more later. Finally, the lower the cost of your future lifestyle, the less you have to save. This is the piece over which you have the most control. Of course, if you are saving more, you are spending less.

For a quick estimate of what you should be setting aside for each $1 million total you need to have saved by the time you retire, use the table on the next page. In the first column is the number of years remaining until you need to have accumulated your total savings. The top row has different time frames with today as a starting point for your short- and mid-term goals, and the remaining rows show how much you should have saved by the end of each time frame starting with no savings. If you save the monthly goal every month, you will meet all the other goals given the assumed rate of return of 7 percent.

The table illustrates why beginning to save as soon as possible is important. The monthly savings requirement more than doubles for every ten years you delay. Early savings is worth more than later savings because your money works for you longer. Your investment returns have investment returns. The first $264 saved grows to $5,500 in forty-five years. The same amount grows to only $728 in fifteen years.

Time Remaining to Retirement	Total Saved In:			
	1 Month	1 Year	5 Years	10 Years
45	$264	$3,300	$18,900	$45,700
35	$555	$6,900	$39,700	$96,100
30	$820	$10,200	$58,700	$141,900
25	$1,234	$15,300	$88,400	$213,700
20	$1,920	$23,800	$137,400	$332,300
15	$3,155	$39,100	$225,900	$546,100

Note: Assumes a 7.0 percent annual rate of return. In 1-, 5-, and 10-year time periods, amounts are rounded to the nearest $100.

These savings estimates are just to get you started. Over time your lifestyle and your income will change, and you'll need to adjust. Don't worry too much about being exactly right. Getting in the ballpark will have you going in the right direction.

Making a big change in your lifestyle immediately to increase your savings may actually be impossible if not merely difficult. But you probably can make small changes and gradually increase your savings to meet your long-term goals.

Small changes can make a big difference. A friend told me about her grandmother who without fail put five dollars in a savings account each week. When she passed away, she had $200,000 in her savings account. Using Bengen's 4 percent rule, that would be worth an extra $666 per month in retirement.

Priorities

Just having a goal isn't enough; it must be your priority. Otherwise it will be too easy to set it aside when something appealing comes along. If you know what your goals will take, you will know how your choices impact your ability to meet them. You can certainly change or reprioritize your goals, but it's important to understand what you give up when you do so.

Years ago, Jeff was managing a building project in the nearby community of Hood River, Oregon, when he fell in love with the area. It's not hard to see why. The community is on the Columbia River in the heart of the scenic Columbia River Gorge. Some locations have amazing mountain and river views, and Hood River is a charming little town with lots of restaurants and boutique shops. One day he suggested we buy a vacation home there.

We could afford a vacation home, but there was a lot to consider. Mortgage payments, taxes, and maintenance on a second home would reduce how much we could save, and that could jeopardize our early retirement goal. That is okay. Nothing says goals can't change. It is all about doing what makes you happy. Was there a way to have both? Was the vacation home really what we wanted?

To get both, we would need to offset the expenses of the second home somehow. One way to offset the additional expenses would be to commit to always vacation in Hood River, eliminating all other vacation expenses, but that wasn't attractive to either of us. We could rent out our vacation home to help cover the costs, but that wasn't a certain source of income, and it would preclude any spontaneous trips to the Gorge. So that wasn't high on our list of options either.

If the vacation home were truly important to us, we could simply decide to take the chance that we would have to work longer than we had originally planned. When I brought up the idea that we might work longer, the conversation came to a screeching halt. Jeopardizing our early retirement goal was a nonstarter. We both decided being able to leave work no later than our midfifties was more important than having a permanent weekend getaway spot. We still happily have only one fully paid-off home.

You can't do everything, so you must make choices. Comparing choices directly can be very illuminating. Vacation home or early retirement? I'll take early retirement. For you, the answer might be vacation home. There is no right or wrong answer.

Dreams Other Than Financial Security

Financial security is just one of your goals. You have other dreams, and there is no reason you can't have dreams and financial security. You have to prepare to realize your dreams financially as thoroughly as you prepare in other ways. And your financial security must remain a priority.

There are so many stories about people following their dreams to financial ruin. To avoid that, understand your trade-offs, make your choices among them deliberately, and set limits. Answer these questions before you set off in pursuit of a dream.

1. What specifically is your dream? Use the SMART (specific, measurable, attainable, realistic, and with a timeframe) goal framework.
2. What is involved in making your dream come true? What steps will you take? How much money will you need? Will you fund it with savings or debt or both? How long will it take to make your dream come true?
3. To make your dream come true, what do you have to stop doing? Will you have to make up for lost time or money later because of what you stopped?

4. How will pursuit of your dream impact your current lifestyle
   and family? Is it worth it?

Pursuing a dream can involve not saving for the future, dig-
ging into savings, or even taking on debt. All these have consequences for which you will need to compensate. You may need
to save more in the future or work longer. You may have to give
up or adjust your other financial goals or even your way of life.

Make these choices up front. It will allow you to evaluate what
you are giving up in order to do what you are taking on and decide whether it's worth it. You wouldn't want to be surprised by
the need to make decisions like these, and you wouldn't want to
look back after the fact wishing you had done things differently.

Often pursuit of a dream involves risk. Money and more could
be lost if things don't work out. Knowing how much you are willing to risk is an important part of preparing. Before you take a
step forward, know what you will do when you reach that limit,
and stick with your decision.

Pursuing a dream while ensuring you don't go broke in the
process can mean big changes in the way you live now as well
as in the future. If these changes seem like sacrifices, it could be
that you aren't as passionate about your pursuit as you thought.
It's better to understand this now rather than later when you
have few choices.

If you have thought through all these issues and your dream
is still your top priority, then go for it. While answering these
questions, you will have created a detailed plan, and with a detailed plan, you will be far more likely to succeed. If you don't go
through this process, you may flail around wasting money and
trying one thing then another. Without a course of action, your
dream is unlikely to materialize.

Chance

Chance and Renée were just about to plop a down payment on a Silicon Valley home when they began to question whether they really wanted to be trapped in "that" life—the one where a house payment chains you to a corporate job that you eventually grow to hate.

Chance dreamed about a life where he and Renée could work from anywhere. They would be globetrotters providing services to businesses around the world. It didn't seem far-fetched. Search the internet, and you'll find stories of successful entrepreneurs living anywhere they please and making a living with nothing but their laptops.

With the hope of creating that alternative lifestyle, Chance and Renée decided not to buy the house. They sold everything they owned, cashed in their company stock options, and quit their corporate jobs. All in, they netted $150,000. They planned to spend $100,000 traveling for a year. Ideally along the way, they would establish some business that would allow them to work from anywhere in the world with plenty of downtime for family and fun. In case it didn't work out, they set aside $50,000 for a reentry fund.

They packed up their two young kids and traveled through India. On the trip, they spent more than they expected and never did do any planning for their business. At the end of eight months, their travel money was gone, and they returned to the States with no alternative lifestyle, no jobs, and no business. They did have their reentry fund though.

They didn't have a specific goal for their life stateside. Chance felt he was fundamentally changed by his travel experience and couldn't return to the corporate lifestyle, but they seemingly had plenty of money to sort things out. Both Chance and Renée tried their hands at a variety of small entrepreneurial ventures. In the meantime, they were living like they had full-time jobs.

Fast-forward two years, and Chance and Renée had still not developed a sustainable business. After plowing through their reentry fund, they blew through $70,000 of retirement savings. Then it was on to the credit cards. Their debts climbed to $125,000. They were in their early forties and didn't own a home. They had no retirement or college savings, and they had an overwhelming amount of high-interest credit card debt.

Today, Chance and Renée have new corporate jobs, and they are trying to rebuild their lives.

Dreams and financial security are not mutually exclusive. It is possible to follow your passion, whatever it is, while still making sure you have the financial wherewithal to support yourself when you can no longer work. But to make that possible, your financial security must be one of your priorities.

Main Ideas

1. While saving money is hard, if you are saving toward a goal, it becomes much easier. Changes you make don't seem like sacrifices. They become steps toward achieving your goal.

2. Creating SMART goals increases your chances of achieving them. SMART goals are specific, measurable, attainable, realistic and have a time frame.

3. Breaking large, long-term goals, like retirement savings goals, down into short- and medium-term goals makes pursuing your goals more manageable.

4. The 4 percent rule is a rule of thumb for estimating how much you can withdraw from your savings and have your savings last for at least 30 years. You will need 25 times your annual withdrawals in savings. Another way to look at it is you can withdraw $333 per month for every $100,000 you have in savings.

5. Your dreams beyond financial security are possible as long as financial security is one of your goals.

Savings Goal Worksheet

Complete this worksheet for each of your savings goals.

In a few words, what is your savings goal?

Write down what you will do to achieve your goal. Be detailed and specific.

Money is the primary measurement tool for savings goals. Describe your goal in terms of money. Break it down into short-, mid- and long-term milestones.

What will you need to attain your goal? What resources will help you?

Why is this goal important to you?

Assign dates for when you will reach your milestones.

Chapter 5

The B-Word: Budgets

NOW THAT YOU HAVE SPECIFIC FINANCIAL GOALS, IT'S TIME TO figure out how to reach them. If you want to take control over your spending so you can save for the important things in your life, you need to have a plan. In other words, you need a budget.

Many see a budget as a kind of diet for your money. You give up something for a while so you can get back on track. Just as you would give up desserts to lose a few pounds, you cut back on some way you spend money to make up for an expense you hadn't planned.

Diets are short term in nature and have been shown to have limited success in helping you lose weight permanently. Once you've lost the weight you planned to lose, you go back to your old eating habits, and before long it's all back. A much more effective approach is to adopt healthy habits that include changing your philosophy and choices about eating and exercise throughout your life.

Similarly, an effective budget reflects your philosophy and choices about spending money throughout your life. It reflects your goals. With a budget, you can avoid spending money in ways that are not important to you and focus on those that are. You are able to reach your financial goals because they are integrated into what you do every month.

Where Does It All Go? Assessing How You Spend

If you want to change the way you spend your money so you have room to save for your financial goals, you first need to figure out where you currently spend it. In chapter 4, you calculated how much you spend overall. Now you need to dig into the nitty-gritty details of what specifically you spend your money on.

Some expenses are easy to identify. You know how much you spend for housing and utilities each month. You might have a ballpark idea of what you spend on groceries, but off the top of your head, you might not get even that right. Beyond the things you get a monthly statement for, you may not have an accurate picture of where your money goes.

To get one, review your spending over the last six months. You can gather this information from your credit card and bank statements. Many card companies and banks help you break down your spending into surprisingly accurate categories based on whom you paid. If they don't do it for you, you'll have to do it yourself.

Typical expense categories include housing, transportation, food, and so on. The following list will help you get started thinking about where your money goes. Add others that might apply to you.

Housing	Mortgage or rent, electricity, gas, water and sewer, cable, trash, maintenance, supplies, etc.
Transportation	Car payment, bus/taxi fare, parking, license and registration, gas, maintenance, etc.
Childcare	Daycare, babysitters, after-school activities, etc.
Insurance	Health, life, car, home
Communication	Phones, cable, internet

Food	Groceries, dining out
Pets	Food, veterinarians, grooming, toys, etc.
Personal care	Medical, hair, clothing, dry cleaning, health club, etc.
Entertainment	Movies, music, concerts, theater, etc.
Nonmortgage loans	Credit card, personal, student, etc.
Gifts	Family, friends, charities
Travel	Vacations
Taxes	Additional federal, state, and local taxes beyond what's taken out of your pay; property taxes
Savings	Emergency fund, retirement, college, etc.

Categorizing your expenses over the last six months will help you include those you might not otherwise remember and set more realistic targets for future spending. If you don't have enough information from the prior months to break down where your money goes, then track it going forward for a few months. Once you have a handle on your regular spending patterns, you'll need to project future expenses to get a complete understanding of the details of your total cost of living.

If you have a family, a car, a house, a deductible on your health care plan, or are otherwise human, you will have expenses that don't show up every month but can be predicted if you think about them.

- Family: Think about upcoming events like holidays, weddings, or anniversaries. Will you need to give a gift, have an unusually expensive dinner, or travel? Will you need to provide a parent or child with financial support?

- Car: A quick look at the owner's manual will tell you when more expensive preventive maintenance is due. Online resources, like Edmunds, can provide estimates of annual maintenance. As your car ages, the cost of maintaining it rises.

- Home: The age of your furnace and other appliances or the time since you last painted are good indicators of upcoming expenses. A good rule of thumb for home repairs is one dollar per square foot per year. You might not spend that every year, but you will eventually. You may also have property taxes, other local taxes, or homeowners' association dues that hit you once a year.

- Health care: Increasingly, health care plans have high deductibles. So there is a good chance that you will pay something out of pocket if you get sick or injured.

Leaving out the expenses that didn't show up every month was a particular problem for Suri. She had tracked her expenses for the last year. She knew exactly where her paycheck was spent, and it looked like she had an extra $450 a month. But somehow she couldn't get a handle on her debt, and each year, despite multiple attempts to pay it down, it got bigger.

Suri had some large expenses that came up annually, which she knew about but wasn't including in her monthly spending assessment. In total she paid over $5,400 in taxes and homeowners' association dues at the end of each year. If she divided that annual expense across the months, she used up her $450 monthly surplus. She didn't really have that money to spend, which was why her debt continued to grow.

These kinds of expenses, if you don't anticipate them, can make it seem futile to create a budget or try to save for the future. They pop up and wipe out your savings when you least expect it. But if you project them and include them in your expenses, you will have a much more robust picture of the cost of your lifestyle. That will enable you to more accurately make changes to your spending so your savings stay saved.

Where Do You Want It to Go? Create Your Budget

With your savings goal in mind, now is the time to start thinking about your philosophy of spending. You will need to decide which activities and experiences are important to you and which are not. You will want to maximize the money available for the important things, including your goals, by minimizing spending on the things you don't value. You may not get this quite right the first time around, but as you work with your budget, you will naturally fine-tune where you want your money to go.

If you have debt payments that are consuming too much of your income or you want to quickly establish a financial cushion, you may want to consider some temporary measures to allow you to make progress faster. Serious cuts in nonessential spending for a short time can allow you to get a jump on your goals. But long-term, your budget won't be successful in helping you reach your goals if your only tool is deprivation. For your budget to work, you must have a clear understanding of your values and priorities.

The following steps will help you get started on your budget:

1. Choose a time increment for your budget. It might be a week, a pay period, or a month.

2. Assign every dollar of income to either meet your spending needs or your savings goals. Tag money not only to go toward your expenses for that time period but also to cover upcoming expenses. If you're going to need new tires soon, specifically put aside money to go toward paying for them. If you have a once-a-year expense, divide the estimated amount by the number of time periods in a year. Set aside a little money each period for that expense.

3. Since you will be accumulating money not only for your savings goals but also for your future expenses, consider opening one or two separate accounts for the money: one for your future expenses and one for your savings goals. If you don't open separate accounts, track the money and its purpose on a spreadsheet or in a budgeting tool (more on tools shortly).

4. Track your spending versus your budget, but don't worry too much about mistakes. Overspending in one area can be offset by lower spending in another area. If the tires cost more than you thought they would, you will need to decide what you can spend less on. The objective is to meet your savings goals and avoid adding to your debt.

To see how predicting future expenses and saving for your goals can change how you spend your money, go to chapter 13. There, I've created an example budget using a real family's expenses that allows them to save for emergencies and upcoming expenses as well as eliminate debt and save for their goals.

You may need to make some adjustments to your budget while you get a handle on your spending. There is nothing wrong with that, and as you get the hang of it, there will be fewer

Cole and Charlotte

Cole and Charlotte were very frustrated with their finances. They felt, between the two of them, that they made decent money. Yet they couldn't manage to save for a down payment on a house. Every month was a juggling act to pay the bills and avoid adding to their debt load.

They had considered taking out a low- or no-down-payment mortgage, but given their budget constraints, they weren't in a position to be homeowners. Even if they could get a mortgage with payments similar to their rent, they would still have to pay property taxes, insurance, and maintenance costs that they weren't currently paying and couldn't afford.

Cole and Charlotte hadn't sorted out their priorities, and they definitely had not elevated saving to one of them. To get a handle on things, they did a six-month assessment of where their money was going. A good chunk of their monthly income was taken up by debt payments, but another good chunk was taken up by things that really didn't provide value to the couple.

For example, their bundled cable package included a land phone line, but they didn't have a phone hooked up to it. They were also surprised by how much they were spending on clothes and eating out. There were several expenses they could reduce or cut out completely if they were willing to pay attention to how they were spending their money.

Before Cole and Charlotte could begin to save for a home, they needed to create some flexibility in their monthly spending. They needed to reduce their debt. If they could make extra payments on their debt, they could quickly bring down the balance that they owed.

With the details of where their money was going, they could decide which expenses were less important to them. By prioritizing debt reduction over spending and creating a plan for how they would spend their money, they could raise enough to make extra payments on their debt. Once that was gone, the money they were using to make debt payments could go to raising a down payment for a house.

adjustments. If your money is tight, it's okay to start with a small goal. Just saving something while being intentional about what you spend will help get you in the habit of saving. You can save more over time.

Tools

There are many tools available to help you plan how you spend and save your money. Many are free online. They will pull information directly from your accounts and consolidate it in a single place. They will provide tutorials to help you get started. They will give you a place to build a budget, and some will send you warnings when you're in danger of violating it or reminders to deposit money in savings.

These are great. But there are other low-tech methods that are just as effective. One simple approach is to segregate your money into separate buckets. You can do this with cash and envelopes, separate bank accounts, or even just separate accounts in a spreadsheet. If you are just getting started, you may benefit from some real, physical separation.

Organizing what your money is intended for is a good way to make sure you aren't spending the mortgage money on something else. It also helps you focus spending your money on things that are important to you while spending less on those that are not.

If you run short in one category, you can more easily make decisions about where to spend less. Not enough money in the "tires" category and driving around with no tread? Take some money from the entertainment or clothing category.

The online tools accomplish the same thing as low-tech alternatives by helping you plan and organize your spending. Of the online tools available, a couple that work well are Mint.com and YouNeedaBudget.com (YNAB). Mint is free.[97] It can pull together information from any of your accounts where you have internet access, allowing you to see your financial information in one place. It also has free budgeting tools and automatic categorization of your expenses. Mint also provides access to other services for a fee, like bill paying and investment management for your savings.

Similarly, YNAB allows you to pull all your financial information together in a single place and provides services, like bill paying. However, YNAB provides a higher level of guidance in creating and sticking with a budget, and for that you pay a fee of $6.99 per month or $83.99 per year.[98] Their approach embraces the concept of giving your money a job so that you can take control of it rather than having the vagaries of life dictate how you spend your money. The subscription provides access to tutorials and classes, and their tools help you stay on track with alerts too.

No tool, however high- or low-tech, is going to do the work for you. You still have to do the hard work of understanding your spending habits and setting up a system that works for you. You also must make the tough decisions about your limits. But the investment is well worth it. The return is the ability to spend your money in the ways that are important to you as well as save for your financial security.

Pay Yourself First

For some, simply making the money unavailable to spend is all it takes to make your savings goal. If you don't see the money, you are less likely to miss it. To take money that you want to save out of contention, take advantage of automation. Evidence from the retirement plan industry shows this works.

A growing trend in corporate retirement plans is automatic enrollment, where employees only have to choose if they don't want to be in the plan. In contrast, the traditional way for employees to enter their retirement plan is to actively sign up for it. With automatic enrollment, employees are enrolled at a preset contribution rate and invested in a default investment option, like a balanced mutual fund (one that invests in a mix of stocks and bonds). Of course, employees can change the contribution rate up or down, or opt out altogether.

In plans that offer auto enrollment, there is higher participation than in plans without it, and fewer than 10 percent of employees opt out of their savings plans even after several years.[99] Less than 15 percent of workers have access to an auto enrollment feature in their plan,[100] but it is becoming increasingly common. The low opt-out numbers indicate that workers don't miss the money once it's taken out of their pay.

Even if your company doesn't use auto enrollment, it isn't difficult to enroll. If your company offers a 401(k) or similar savings plan, sign up. If not, there are other automated ways to save. Most employers offer to direct deposit your pay, and they often have the ability to send your money to more than one account. You can have some of your pay automatically deposited to an individual retirement or other savings account.

If direct deposit isn't available to you, most banks will do automatic transfers on a schedule you determine. Have your bank transfer your target savings to your savings account on a regular basis. If the money is tucked away before you have a chance at it, you're likely to adapt to the money that you do have, and your savings will grow.

Rules of Your Road

An effective way to get yourself into the saving habit is to create rules for yourself. While these are low barriers to spending your money, they can help you establish new and better habits.

A Portland, Oregon, financial counselor, Shell Tain, told me a story about a young man who earned what most would consider a generous professional salary. He just couldn't figure out how he could save money. He was spending everything he brought home. Shell challenged him to take $200 cash out of his bank account each week and live on that alone.

Beyond his rent and utility payments, all his expenses—gas, groceries, entertainment, whatever—were to come out of the $200. The first week he struggled to make the money last. But it wasn't long before his expenses stayed well within the cash limit. In fact, he found he had money left over at the end of each week once he got in the swing of things. He was saving money.

Other rules might include only having lunch or coffee out one day per week. Or setting a date night and only having dinner out on that night. Making these expenses events can make them more meaningful while preventing you from going over budget.

If carrying cash has you spending more rather than less, only carry cash when you know you need to buy something that is in your budget. Then only carry enough cash to cover it. If credit cards are your nemesis, put them somewhere that is hard to get.

A safe-deposit box at the bank. A block of ice in your freezer. A compartment in your attic. Wherever it will take a bit of extra effort for you to get at them can be a good place.

Another way to curb your impulses is to impose a cooling-off period for yourself. If you are tempted to buy something, give yourself twenty-four hours to think it over. The time will let you figure out whether there is room in your budget and whether it truly is your priority.

Find a strategy that works for you. If you are ready to prioritize saving over spending, you will be able to create a plan and reach your goals. Sure, there will be setbacks. Don't beat yourself up. Make the adjustments that you need to make and move forward. Once you get the hang of it, saving will become a lifestyle. You won't be able to stop being conscientious about how you spend your money. You will know too much.

Only You Know How You Should Spend Your Money

When my friends found out I was working on a book about saving money, they became a little self-conscious around me. One friend bowed her head when telling me about the specialty carpet she was installing. She said, "Julie, I know, I'm never going to be able to retire." Of course she was joking, but people tend to think that the only way to financial security is to give up things that don't fit into the traditionally wise uses for your money.

You don't have to give up the things that are important to you to achieve financial security. You wouldn't be very happy if you did. Depriving yourself of what you really enjoy can keep you from a long-term commitment to healthy saving habits. But you do need to prioritize and understand your trade-offs.

Lisa and Candice loved to go out. They liked eating at restaurants or going to a club to listen to music. It was an important part of what made them happy. Yet when they wanted to take control of their money, pay down debt, and save for the future, the first thing they thought they had to give up was going out.

That was a sure way to sabotage their efforts. It's hard to stick with anything when you give up something that's important to you. Life is about making choices, but it's not necessarily a choice between a secure financial future and doing what you love.

For most it can be a choice between financial security and not doing what you don't love. Many spend money on things that are neither required nor meaningful to them. For couples like Lisa and Candice, there are alternatives to giving up date nights.

For instance, they could give up less-meaningful restaurant trips, like daily coffee or takeout lunch that they eat at their desk. They could lower the cost of their cable package or something else. Perhaps they could find a lower-cost way to enjoy a night out. It may even be that they go out less often if they want to meet their goals, but that doesn't mean they can't go out at all.

Your budget should reflect what you value. Build in the things that are important to you. Just understand that you will give up something else in the process, and choose wisely. Give up the things that don't bring you safety, security, or joy, and make sure saving for your future is among the things you keep.

Main Ideas

1. A budget is a plan for how you want to spend your money, not a diet for it.
2. The first step in making a plan is figuring out where you are. Assess how you currently spend your money, and make sure to include those expenses that don't come up every month, like maintenance, taxes, family obligations, and health care.

3. Build your budget by assigning every dollar of income to either an expense or saving.
4. Take whatever steps necessary, whether it's stashing money away before you see it or creating rules for how you will behave, to help you stick with your budget.
5. Make your budget your own. Only you know your values and priorities.

The following budget template captures most spending categories for the typical household. Use it to get started on your own spending plan.

Budget Worksheet

Total monthly income	

HOUSING	Projected Cost
Mortgage or rent	
Phone	
Electricity	
Gas	
Water and sewer	
Cable/internet	
Waste removal	

HOUSING	Projected Cost
Maintenance or repairs	
Supplies	
Other	
Subtotal	

TRANSPORTATION	Projected Cost
Vehicle payment	
Bus/taxi fare	
Insurance	
Licensing	
Fuel	
Maintenance	
Other	
Subtotal	

INSURANCE	Projected Cost
Home	
Health	
Life	

INSURANCE	Projected Cost
Other	
Subtotal	

FOOD	Projected Cost
Groceries	
Dining out	
Other	
Subtotal	

PETS	Projected Cost
Food	
Medical	
Grooming	
Toys	
Other	
Subtotal	

PERSONAL CARE	Projected Cost
Medical	
Hair/nails	

PERSONAL CARE	Projected Cost
Clothing	
Dry cleaning	
Health club	
Other	
Subtotal	

ENTERTAINMENT	Projected Cost
Video/DVDs/CDs	
Movies	
Concerts/sporting events	
Live theater	
Other	
Subtotal	

LOANS	Projected Cost
Personal	
Student	
Credit card	
Other	

LOANS	Projected Cost
Subtotal	

GIFTS AND DONATIONS	Projected Cost
Charity 1	
Charity 2	
Subtotal	

TAXES	Projected Cost
Federal	
State	
Property	
Other	
Subtotal	

SAVINGS OR INVESTMENTS	Projected Cost
Retirement account	
Other	
Subtotal	

Total Costs Should Equal Total Income	

Chapter 6

Cutting Your Expenses

YOUR BUDGET IS A ZERO-SUM GAME. SHORT OF EARNING MORE money, you only have so much of it to spread around. If you spend money on one thing, you have less to spend on others or save. You can buy lattes every day at the coffee shop or skip them and in three months have enough for a weekend getaway. Or over a year you can add $1,500 to your IRA. If you want to increase your savings, you have to make some choices. In this chapter you will find some ideas for cutting your expenses.

Of course, this is not an exhaustive list. You may be able to think of other things. These ideas are also not a judgment about how you should spend your money. You should spend your money in the ways that make you happy. But if you are spending so much that you can't reach your savings goals, consider these options for cutting back.

Low-Hanging Fruit

Look for things that you pay for but don't use. Many people are stuck in a loop of paying for things either because those things came with something they do use or because an automatic payment was set up at some point in the past. This is low-hanging fruit for getting your budget on track and doing all the things you know you should be doing financially. All it takes is asking yourself when the last time was that you used these services or things. Here are a few areas to think about to get the ball rolling.

- **Your telephone landline:** The cable companies have pushed bundled packages that include telephone, cable, and internet services. If your primary phone is your cell phone, you can save by dropping the phone service.
- **Premium cable channels:** You may have signed up for the premium cable channels when you had cable installed. Maybe they came free with the installation, and now the free period is over. Whether it's because you don't have time or you're using Netflix to stream your favorite movies, you're not watching those premium channels. Going to a less expensive package could save you. Dropping TV and phone, leaving just internet, could save you even more if you substitute streaming services to get your favorite shows.
- **Cell phone services:** Service contracts often include things you don't need. For example, one carrier was offering 20 GB of data for $80 per month. That sounds great, but do you really use 20 GB of data in a month? Check your statement to see how much you really use, and then see if you can make any easy changes. Consider adjusting your data subscription to what you actually do use. You may be able to reduce the data you use if you keep data-heavy activities, like playing games or streaming, to times when Wi-Fi is available. Wi-Fi is available in so many places now that this might not be much of a sacrifice.
- **Cell phone carrier:** Companies like Verizon, Sprint, T-Mobile, and AT&T spend a lot on advertising, but they are far from

the only games in town. Several small providers offer better deals and use the same networks as the big four.

- **Gym memberships:** The average gym membership costs $58 per month, yet two-thirds of people with memberships never use them.[101] If you use your gym membership, great, but if you don't, you won't miss it if you cancel it.

- **Magazine subscriptions:** Perhaps you subscribed to a magazine or two to help your neighbor's kid raise money for their school. Do those find their way to the recycling bin without you giving them a second glance? Then there is no need to renew them. Make sure they don't auto renew if you put the subscription on your credit card.

- **Income taxes:** Do you regularly get an income tax refund? In the 2015 tax filing season, nearly three-quarters of filers received a refund, and the average amount was almost $2,800. According to the IRS, these numbers are fairly consistent from year to year.[102] If you get a refund, it means you paid too much. You don't even get good karma from lending the IRS your hard-earned money for the year. Instead of paying an extra $233 per month to the government, you could use that money to add to your retirement savings or bolster your emergency fund.

These are just a few areas where you can look for savings without having to give anything up or even put in much effort beyond the initial investment of time. With a little more effort, there are savings to be had in your day-to-day spending as well.

Slightly Higher-Hanging Fruit

The latest available data from the US Department of Agriculture (2014) indicates Americans spend about 10 percent of their disposable income on food,[103] with average annual spending running near $6,800.[104] About 56 percent of the food budget is spent at the grocery store, and 44 percent is spent on food away from home—or in other words, eating out. Food may be a good place to look for some savings. Possibilities include eating out less and lowering your grocery bill.

Eating Out

Nationwide, Americans eat out 4.5 times per week and, when eating out for dinner, spend about $39 per person.[105] The thought of eating out is enticing for so many reasons. It's fun to get out of the house and into a new environment. It's great to get out of cooking and cleaning. We long to eat something special, something different, attractive, and delicious. Or sometimes it just seems convenient to go out.

Eating out, regardless of the meal, is a budget killer. It's the convenience meals that you want to cut out. They aren't as convenient as you might think.

If you have a meal planned and have all the ingredients on hand, you can have a fresh, delicious dinner ready in no more than half an hour. If you consider the time it takes to drive to a restaurant, park or drive through, wait to have your order taken, wait for your food to be prepared, and drive home, you could easily chew up a half an hour or more.

Eating out socially is the other main reason for going to a restaurant. There's something about catching up with friends or your special someone over a meal. If you plan your evenings out, you'll have a handle on what you can afford before you go, and you are likely to enjoy it even more. You don't always have to go out to have the social experience. Invite your friends over and have them contribute to the meal. You'll all save money.

Eating at Home

Food at home can be just as attractive and delicious as food at a restaurant, and it doesn't necessarily take more time. Our family eats out only occasionally. For me, it's frustrating to see how expensive food in restaurants can be, especially when Jeff is such a great cook. But with access to the internet, anyone can learn how to make great food at home. If you're more adventurous, you can just wing it and do well.

Even our daughter, Kaye, has become a good cook. One of Kaye's chores was to make dinner for Jeff and me on Sunday evenings. It seemed only fair, since we made dinner for her the other six days of the week. Since Kaye, like most teenagers, wasn't much of a planner, Sunday meals were usually made from whatever we happened to have on hand when she started thinking about dinner at 4:00 p.m. Fortunately, our kitchen is well stocked.

Eating at home doesn't need to be routine, dull, or time consuming. With a little planning, you can have a fantastic meal for a fraction of the cost of going out. To keep your meal prep time down on busy days, consider cooking a few meals ahead on your days off so you have something you can just warm when time is short. Or you can get your kids to cook for you.

Make a Grocery Shopping List

There are easy ways to save money at the grocery store too. A recent study found as much as 30 percent of your dollars could be going to things you didn't plan on buying.[106] But many of these purchases could be going to waste. One startling statistic is that American households throw out a quarter of the food they buy.[107] If you could reduce your grocery bill by 25 to 30 percent, you could make a meaningful contribution to savings. To capture these savings and reduce the amount of food you waste at the same time, make a list before you go to the grocery store.

For a good list you can stick with, start with your calendar. Your calendar shows you what you have on the docket for the coming week, and that will help you know how much time you have for making food. Days where there is soccer practice or a meeting at your kid's school are days when you have less time to prepare meals, and your meal preparation needs to be simplified. Don't forget your work schedule. Will someone in the house be traveling, working late, or otherwise not be at home for meals?

Next come up with a menu for the week that fits with your calendar. Meals that need more preparation should be saved for days when you have less going on, and simple meals or meals you can prepare ahead are for your busy days. You have a menu for what your family is going to eat, and it fits with the time you have to make it.

Last, make your list. Using your menu, review what you have on hand already. Then add missing ingredients to your list. Now you have a list that will ensure you have everything you need for the coming week.

Because you created a menu, you won't be as tempted by off-list items. You know exactly what you need, and there is no reason to buy something just in case. Because you reviewed your inventory, you won't have to guess whether you already have something, saving you from double buying. Finally, because you have a known purpose for everything you buy, you will throw out less.

Other Grocery Store Strategies

Beyond the list there are a few other grocery store strategies that can save you money. Changing the store where you shop, staying away from prepackaged foods, and shopping sales all offer worthwhile savings.

There can be a large disparity in the prices that grocery stores charge. There are the high-end stores like Whole Foods, there are discount grocers, and several in between. Our local news outlet here in Portland did a comparison of seven chains in the metro area on a list of five common grocery items. There was a difference of 30 percent between the highest-priced store and the lowest-priced store.[108]

The prospect of saving almost a third on your grocery bill is an incentive to at least check out your alternatives. Even if you are shopping organic or have other specialty food requirements, you may be surprised at the selection offered by the lower-cost grocery stores.

Another grocery store savings trick is to avoid paying for packaging. The more that goes into making food portable and presentable, the more it costs. If you can slice it, divide it, or put it in your own container, you will save. In many cases, just a few extra minutes of your time can give you all the advantages offered by the packaged products and save you lots of money. The following table compares a few packaged food items to their unpackaged alternatives.

Prepackaged		Unpackaged	
Bottled ice tea (6 pack)	$9.89	Home-brewed ice tea (same volume)	$1.00
Steel-cut oatmeal (24 oz package)	$3.00	Bulk steel-cut oats (24 oz)	$0.60

Prepackaged		Unpackaged	
GoGo squeeZ applesauce (12 pack)	$8.79	Applesauce (same volume)	$3.84
McCormick ground cinnamon (2.4 oz)	$2.37	Bulk cinnamon (2.4 oz)	$0.58
Sliced apples (five 2 oz multipacks)	$4.49	Apples (10 oz)	$2.18

The final tool for squeezing every last penny out of your grocery store visit is couponing and shopping the sales. Carrie Rocha manages a website, www.pocketyourdollars.com, with a coupon database and currently running deals at a variety of national chain stores. She also wrote the book *Pocket Your Dollars: 5 Attitude Changes That Will Help You Pay Down Debt, Avoid Financial Stress, and Keep More of What You Make.* She advocates shopping the sales and claims that you can shave 30 to 40 percent off your grocery bill if you buy what you use when it is on sale instead of when you need it.[109]

The grocery store is designed to get you to buy as much stuff as possible. The arrangement of the food and displays has been scientifically proven to increase your total spending at the store. But with a little planning and a rethink of how and where you buy your food, there are big savings to be had.

Take Care of Your Stuff

Spending a little money on a regular basis can save you lots of money in the long run. An important way to save money on big-ticket items is to take care of them. Whether it's your furnace, your water heater, your roof, or your car, paying for the regular maintenance will make them last longer and help you avoid dealing with their unexpected demise.

Today's cars have a long life. A well-maintained car will last 200,000 miles or more. But you can chop 50,000 miles off that estimate if you don't perform the regular maintenance on it.[110]

Home appliances never fail when it's cheap and easy to replace them. They fail at the worst possible time because that is when you are using them the most. Furnaces don't fail in the summer. They fail in the winter when it's freezing outside because that is when they are working the hardest. Usually it's at night and on the weekend because that's when you're home. Service and replacement at these times is at its most expensive. The same is true for your roof and all the other big things that make your home safe and comfortable.

If you have a system you depend on—such as your furnace, water heater, or car—maintain it. If it is aging, plan to replace it. If you replace it before it fails, you will have the time to find the best replacement for your situation, the best service provider, and the best deal.

The Highest Hanging Fruit

The next level of savings requires more work and harder decisions. While small changes in how you spend your money can add up to big savings, if the previous strategies haven't opened up much flexibility in your spending, you may need to consider more dramatic steps. Housing and transportation are the biggest categories of average household spending, accounting for more than a third of annual expenses.[111] So it's reasonable to look at these for savings.

Housing

Are you house poor? If your house payments, utilities, taxes, insurance, and maintenance costs make it hard for you to save money, then the answer may be yes. You may not even know it because you are able to cover your living expenses from your income and may be enjoying a lovely house in a great neighborhood. But without savings, a single financial setback, such as a job loss, could cause you to lose your home. And you are not preparing for your long-term financial security. Reducing the cost of your housing can go a long way toward making you financially secure.

Janice and her husband made a big change that allowed them to increase their savings. After years of living the suburban lifestyle, they found that a house and a yard really weren't their thing, so they sold. They bought a condominium closer to where they worked for much less than the sale price of their house.

With the extra money, they paid off all their debt (other than their new mortgage). The lower house payments and the elimination of their debt payments allowed them to maximize their 401(k) contributions and begin funding individual retirement accounts.

If your house is more than you need, you may not need to sell it to reduce your housing costs. Theresa was a single professional woman. She had purchased her first home a few years prior. One day, in frustration, she asked how she could possibly save for retirement while making house payments and paying for life in general. Theresa's house payments were swallowing up more of her paycheck than she could afford and still meet her savings goals.

One answer to Theresa's problem would be to take on a roommate. While everyone likes to have their own space, a roommate is a reasonable choice if you don't want to move and need to save more. Given local rents, Theresa could have made $500 per month easily. That would be a nice addition to her retirement savings.

If you are in the market for a new home, don't let the amount of money the mortgage company will loan you drive your price range. Just because you qualify for a loan doesn't make it affordable. Keep in mind that not only will you have a mortgage payment, but you will also have to pay taxes and insurance, and there will inevitably be things to fix.

Start with a monthly payment that you can comfortably afford while meeting your savings goals and leaving room to pay these extra expenses. Then work backward from there. The loan and down payment that deliver that monthly payment determine the home price you can afford. There will be more on mortgages in chapter 7.

Transportation

Beyond housing, the other big-ticket item is transportation, which accounts for almost as much spending for the average household. Owning a car is expensive, and that doesn't even consider how much they cost to buy. There are the operating expenses of gas, maintenance, and tires, and there are the ownership expenses of licensing, registration, taxes, and insurance. If you borrowed money to buy the car, you're paying interest on the loan, and cars decline in value every year.

Each year AAA estimates the annual cost of ownership of different vehicles, taking these expenses into account and given how many miles you drive in a year. The chart on the following page summarizes the information. The average is over $9,500 a year. If you work in an urban area, you may pay for parking, so add another $2,000 to each of the numbers in the chart.

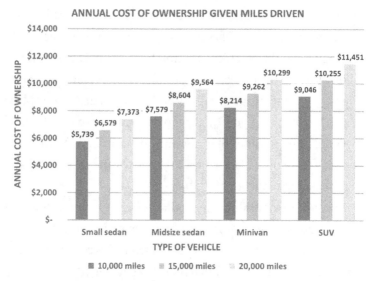

ANNUAL COST OF OWNERSHIP GIVEN MILES DRIVEN

Source: AAA, *Your Driving Costs*

There are a few ways to keep your transportation costs down. The most dramatic is to go without a car. Alternatives to owning a car include taking public transit, carpooling, and working from home. The American Public Transportation Association estimates the average driver could save over two-thirds the cost of owning a car if they switched to public transit.[112]

Not having a car doesn't mean that you are trapped in your city or that you have to lug your groceries home by hand. The availability of subscription car rental services, like car2go and Zipcar, mean that you can get access to a car for a short trip or for the weekend without the ongoing expense of owning a car.

If going without a car isn't an option, make sure you have the right car. At one time we had a Ford Explorer. It was a gas-guzzler, and they aren't cheap. We thought we needed it to haul things if we undertook a landscaping or home repair project. We also

Cecilia

After her divorce, Cecilia was looking for a home of her own. She wanted the stability of having her own place again and a secure environment for her two teenage sons. She and her ex-husband had decided to rent out the family home while the housing market recovered from the financial crisis. Otherwise, the proceeds from selling the house wouldn't cover the mortgage.

Cecilia didn't have a down payment, since she didn't have any equity to pull from the prior house. Because she took the bus to work anyway, she decided to sell her car and use the money she saved to raise a down payment for a new home. She estimated that between payments, insurance, taxes, registration, maintenance, and gas, she would save $14,000 a year.

While the bus was a great way to get to work, that still left grocery shopping and other excursions to deal with. She signed up for car2go for weekend errands. She never had to walk more than a quarter mile to the nearest available car, and she never had to worry about gassing up or parking fees. She also became an avid Uber user, and for her few longer extended trips, she rented a car from Enterprise.

It didn't take Cecilia long to save her down payment, and she now has a home she can see herself living in for the rest of her life. She never replaced her car. The alternatives were convenient enough that she didn't miss owning one. Now her savings from not owning a car go toward her goal of retiring early.

used to camp, and with a daughter and a dog, we thought we needed the space.

But when we really boiled it down, we realized we used the extra space for about 3 percent of our life. So we replaced the Explorer with a Toyota Prius. We decided that on the occasions we needed something bigger, we would rent. As it turns out, we've never done that. The Prius has all the space we need. The nearly $8,000 difference in price was a huge savings, and the thirty to forty extra miles per gallon has also helped.

Another way to limit your transportation costs is to keep your car longer. The average person keeps their car for about eleven years, but your car may have more life left in it. If you drive an average number of miles, your car could last well over fourteen years. If your car doesn't have serious structural problems and it remains reliable with normal maintenance, you can reasonably keep it. Keeping your car longer allows you to spread out your purchase price over more years, and as your car gets older, expenses for insurance and registration go down.

Decisions to change where you live or how you get around are tremendously difficult. But it is decisions like these that make your goals possible. Keeping your lifestyle in line with your goals not only allows you to save more, but it also puts those goals in closer reach. The lifestyle you have to replace simply costs less.

Most of us have choices about how we spend our money, and many of us are spending money in ways that really don't make our lives better. To make a move in the right direction, sometimes all it takes is discovering a few of these. Saving more for your future may be easier than you think.

Main Ideas

1. The first place to look for ways to cut your expenses is in the things that are underused or you don't use at all.
2. Eating out is expensive. Save it for special occasions. Making meals at home can be more convenient and less expensive if you prepare ahead.
3. You can save on groceries by making a shopping list, shopping at a less expensive store, avoiding packaged foods, and shopping sales.
4. Spending money on maintaining your car, home, and appliances will save you money in the end. They will last longer, and you will be less likely to be surprised by expensive, unplanned repair bills.
5. If all else fails to yield the savings you need, look for alternatives to your housing and transportation choices.

Chapter 7

Debt: The Good, the Bad, and the Ugly

DEBT IS AN INSIDIOUS THING. WHILE IT LUBRICATES THE GEARS of society and allows you to accomplish things that would otherwise be difficult, nothing will stand in the way of you reaching your goals like debt. When you take on debt, you are essentially spending tomorrow's money today. Some forms of debt have merit, but all forms of debt take away financial flexibility and reduce your financial security.

Today it's easy to spend money you don't have. Even if you're not planning it, with the swipe of a credit card you can bump your total spending beyond what you take home in a month. Once you have debt, it is a kind of expense that isn't flexible. You can't choose to not pay it, so as debt builds, it crowds out other ways to spend your money. Over time you can spend less and less on things other than debt payments.

Debt can be minimized if you go at life with that intention. If you have debt already, paying it down is a form of savings with a guaranteed return equal to the interest on your loan. More importantly, eliminating debt gives you flexibility. Your cost of living and your need for savings will be lower, giving you the space to do the things that are important to you.

Mortgages

Mortgage loans represent the largest single debt in most households. If you want to own a home, you have little choice but to take out a mortgage. Fortunately, mortgage loans are the cheapest form of debt. Because your home provides security for the lender, mortgage interest rates are low relative to other forms of debt. Mortgage interest is also tax-deductible if your total tax-deductible expenses are greater than the standard deduction for your family.

Thirty-year fixed mortgage interest rates were in the mid- to high 4 percent range in 2018.[113] You have to live somewhere. If you don't own your home, you would be renting. Of course, owning a home comes with lots of other expenses, but over time you pay down the mortgage, and you get an asset that will grow in value. Mortgage debt is a good form of debt.

But even good debt can become bad. Your bank will likely be willing to lend you more than you can afford. Especially in expensive housing markets, like Portland, Seattle, San Francisco, and others, it's tempting to spend as much on a home as the bank is willing to lend you. Your dollar just doesn't go very far in these cities. But that can put you in a precarious position.

You may be thinking that if a bank is willing to lend you the money, you must be able to afford it. But the bank doesn't really care about your other goals or even your financial security. They only care that you can make the payment, and they have a formula that gives them confidence you can. The formula, called the **debt-to-income ratio**, is the biggest factor in determining how much money the bank is willing to lend you.

The debt-to-income ratio is your monthly debt payments divided by your gross monthly income (your income before taxes). Banks generally cap your debt-to-income ratio, including the mortgage payment, at 43 percent.[114] Other factors like your credit score and down payment will influence whether they will lend enough to push your ratio to the full 43 percent. But if you have a good credit score and can put at least 10 percent down, you will likely be eligible for the maximum loan amount.

Think about that for a moment. The bank will lend you up to the amount that makes your total debt payments as much as 43 percent of your income before taxes. You likely only take home between 65 and 70 percent of your gross income after taxes and benefits. You could be paying more than two-thirds of your take-home pay in debt payments. There would be no room for saving for your other financial goals, and if you or your partner lost their job, you could easily lose the house.

Despite your bank's confidence in you, to keep your monthly obligations at a more comfortable level your total debt payments should be no higher than 25 percent of your income. To estimate how much loan you can get away with given the payment you can afford, visit www.financial-calculators.com/mortgage-calculator. This calculator provides the loan amount when you enter the payment you can afford. It doesn't include taxes and insurance, so you'll want to leave room for those. However, it's a good place to start.

Just because you can justify taking out a mortgage loan doesn't mean you shouldn't work to someday be mortgage-free. Paying off your mortgage will improve your financial security significantly and reduce your cost of living. If you have a $1,500 mortgage payment, for example, your cost of living would go down by $18,000 per year if it were paid off.

You will want to be mortgage-free by the time you stop working for pay. Housing expenses for retirees with a mortgage are three times that of those without one. And with equity in your home, you can use it as a backstop should your retirement savings run low. You can either sell the house or take out a **reverse mortgage** to provide you with additional income.

A reverse mortgage is a type of mortgage available to those aged sixty-two and older. When you take out a reverse mortgage, the bank loans you money and expects to get paid back when you ultimately leave the home. Whether the mortgage is taken as a single lump sum, a line of credit, or as monthly payments to you, you do not have to make payments on it. The loan with interest is paid from the proceeds of the sale of the home at some date in the future.

Because the repayment date is uncertain, the loan the bank will be willing to make as a percentage of your total equity will be much lower than a traditional mortgage. If you've paid off your traditional mortgage, it will leave more room to use this tool to bolster your retirement savings. Reverse mortgages can be expensive and should not be plan A for making ends meet in retirement. But if you find your savings running short, they can be a useful tool.

A mortgage is the key to home ownership, and home ownership brings its own security. However, don't buy more home than you can afford, and even though mortgage debt is good debt, it is still well worth paying off. A paid-off home is a very big asset, and the financial flexibility will be important when you are living on your savings.

Auto Loans

Like homes, cars are expensive, and it may be hard to imagine buying one without a loan. Also, as with a home, you do have something to show for your debt, but cars go down in value, not up. Car loans are not bad debt, but they can be avoided.

Car loans range in terms from three to seven years. The average term for an auto loan is sixty-eight months, with seventy-two- and eighty-four-month loans becoming more common. The longer the loan term, the higher the interest rate. Longer loans do offer lower payments; however, the lower payments may not be worth it.

Car values decline rapidly. After only three years, a new car will be worth less than two-thirds of what you paid for it.[115] With longer payment schedules, you could wind up owing more than your car is worth. To avoid that, keep your car loan as short as possible. You will pay less for the car because you will have a lower interest rate paid over a shorter time.

If you keep your car long enough, you can pay cash for your next car. With regular maintenance, cars can remain reliable for 200,000 miles.[116] The average American drives 13,476 miles per year.[117] That means on average you could keep a car for more than fourteen years.

If you buy the car with a five-year loan, then once the car is paid off, you can use the money that was going toward the payment to save for your next car. You'll have enough for the next car long before you need it. For example, if you buy a car for $20,000 with a five-year loan, your payments will be around $350 per month. After the car is paid off, put the $350 in savings. In another five years, you'll have enough money to buy your next car for cash. Better yet, just save enough to buy the first car and skip the loan altogether.

Credit Card Debt

Credit card debt is bad debt. Credit cards have high interest rates, and generally whatever you buy with them will have little to no value to anyone else. Most Americans carry a balance on their credit cards. Only 35 percent pay off their balance every month.[118] Americans who have credit card debt owe an average of $16,883 per household and pay $1,300 per year in interest.[119]

It is so easy to rack up credit card balances. When you whip out your card to pay for something, it's like you didn't even spend any money. If you don't keep track of your credit card purchases, you don't know what you've spent until you get the bill.

Even when you get the bill, the minimum payment isn't very much, so it doesn't hurt to keep the credit rolling. Credit card debt is **revolving**—you don't have a time limit to pay it all back, and whatever you do pay frees up more credit for more purchases.

Credit card companies love it when you carry a balance. They keep their minimum payment low so you can afford to keep charging away. The typical minimum credit card payment is 1 percent of your outstanding balance plus interest charged on any carryover balance, plus fees.[120] Often there will also be a minimum dollar payment of between $10 and $25. Even if you don't charge another dollar, it could take you twenty-eight years to pay off a $16,883 balance if you only make the minimum payment.

If you carry a balance on your credit card from month to month, you are simply spending more than you make. To get your spending under control, give the card a rest. Give yourself an allowance and only pay cash for your daily expenses. It will be more painful to spend money as you watch the cash leaving your wallet. Stay away from browsing internet retailers and unsubscribe to online retailers' emails. In chapter 5 you learned how to create a spending plan that will keep your spending within what you can afford. Later in this chapter, you'll learn a strategy for paying off your debt.

401(k) and Other Retirement Account Loans

Borrowing from your retirement account is also bad debt. While you are essentially borrowing from yourself, there are several consequences to taking the loan that make this a bad idea.

Most retirement plans allow participants to borrow against their balances. About one in five 401(k) participants have an outstanding loan, and over a five-year period, almost 40 percent of participants have had an outstanding loan at some point.[121] Most loans are taken to pay off debt, usually of the credit card variety.[122]

That can make some sense, since the loan rate on a 401(k) loan is lower than rates on credit cards. But there are other costs beyond the interest rate.

- While your loan is outstanding, your money is not invested in the market. You are earning the interest on the loan to yourself, but you are missing out on the greater growth you could get from stock market–oriented investments. The market rate of return is the true cost of your loan. Historically the stock market has returned on average 10 percent per year.

- Some employers don't allow you to make contributions while you have a loan outstanding. If that is the case with your plan, you will miss out on the opportunity to grow your retirement account balance. If your employer matches contributions, you will also miss out on that.

- Your loan is repaid with after-tax dollars. When you retire, the money you repaid, like the rest of your balance, will be taxed when you take it out to meet your living expenses. So your loan will be taxed twice.

- If you leave or are let go from your job, you will only have sixty days to repay the loan or it will be considered a distribution. The distribution will be taxed as ordinary income in the year you take it, and you will pay an additional 10 percent penalty.

In some cases, a loan on your retirement account may be the best of a few bad options, but that doesn't make it a good one. There are costs that aren't obvious, and they put you at risk of a big tax bill if you lose your job.

Student Loans

Student loans are good debt, but they are ugly. By getting an education or certification, you are investing in yourself, and that will pay dividends. Paying for part of your education with debt can be reasonable, and student loans offer flexibility you don't get with other kinds of debt. However, this flexibility is largely misunderstood and can lead to serious financial problems.

Furthering your education or simply acquiring a new skill is a proven way to boost your earning power and keep you employed. The chart on the next page, which uses data from the Bureau of Labor Statistics, shows median weekly earnings and unemployment rates by education level.[123] The higher the level of your education, the higher your earning potential and your chances of remaining employed. If you have a bachelor's degree, you can expect to earn two-thirds more than someone with a high school diploma and face unemployment half as often. Graduate degrees offer even more financial rewards and job security.

It's hard to argue with the merits of getting an education, and tuition and fees are so high that student loans seem inevitable. More than 70 percent of those graduating with a bachelor's degree in 2016 graduated with some student debt.[124] The average

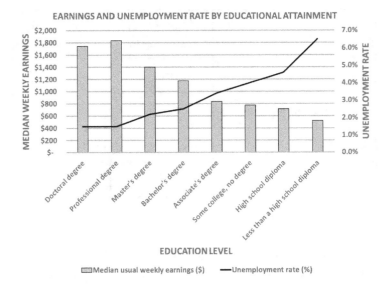

EARNINGS AND UNEMPLOYMENT RATE BY EDUCATIONAL ATTAINMENT

total debt was over $28,000. It's no wonder that student loans are the second-largest category of debt outstanding in America.

Of the more than $1.3 trillion in student loans outstanding, 40 percent was used to finance graduate studies, and it is with graduate programs that the balances really start to balloon. The following table shows the typical balances and payments by graduate degree.

Degree	Average Total Student Debt	Average Monthly Payment
Master of business administration	$42,000	$354
Master of education	$50,879	$429
Master of science	$50,400	$425

Degree	Average Total Student Debt	Average Monthly Payment
Master of arts	$58,539	$494
All other master's degrees	$55,489	$468
Law	$140,616	$1,187
Medicine	$161,772	$1,365

Source: Delisle, *The Graduate Student Debt Review.*

Student loans are easy to get. How else could an eighteen-year-old with no job, collateral, or credit history get tens of thousands in loans? Few students fully grasp the gravity of what they are taking on. A study by the Federal Reserve found that more than half of students who take on student loans do not understand the fundamentals of debt.[125]

Counseling provided before loans are taken generally centers around how much a student can borrow. It isn't until close to graduation, when it is too late, that payments are discussed in conjunction with payment plans. Government-mandated education for student borrowers is provided online, and students spend little time with it.[126]

In addition to these loans being easy to get, you can stop making payments if you are back in school, and recently created repayment plans allow you to pay less than even the interest on your loan in some circumstances. If you return to school for any reason, you may defer payments on your loans while you attend. Though you don't have to make payments, your loan is still accruing interest. That means that every month you don't make a payment, your debt is growing.

If your income makes it hard to make your standard loan payment, you can switch to a plan with **graduated payments** that start low and rise over time. Or you might choose a **Pay As You Earn (PAYE)** payment plan. With the PAYE plans, your loan payment is no more than 10 percent of your discretionary income, which is based on the difference in your family's income after taxes and 150 percent of the government-designated poverty line.

If you have a big debt load, you could easily be paying less than the interest due on your loan. Which, like with deferment, means that with every passing month you are adding to your debt. The PAYE repayment plans allow any unpaid loan amounts you have left to be forgiven after twenty or twenty-five years, depending on when you signed up for the program.[127]

But there is a catch. While your loans may be forgiven by the student loan arm of the government, they won't be forgiven by the IRS. The amount of student loans forgiven will be counted as income in the year it is forgiven, increasing your taxable income. In the extreme, if your debt is high and your income low, you may not be able to afford the tax bill.

There is one other way for your loans to be forgiven without the tax nightmare. If you go to work for a qualifying nonprofit or government employer, your loans could be forgiven, with no tax consequences, after ten years of service through the **Public Service Loan Forgiveness Program.**

Loan deferrals, flexible payment plans, and easy money make student loans dangerous territory. Half of borrowers don't begin repaying their loans until they are in their midthirties, and 30 percent are not reducing their balances after five years of payment.[128] Large loan balances cause students to forgo home ownership and postpone saving for retirement.

With the high cost of education, it may seem like debt is unavoidable, but there are things that you can do to at least minimize it. They aren't easy, but they are worth it for your financial security.

- Save ahead to cover part of your expenses. Know the full cost of your degree program, including tuition and fees. Set a time frame for starting your program, and save as much money as you can toward your education before you start. Saving toward your education will help with the next piece of advice as well.
- Live frugally while you are in school. If you were already saving to help fund your education, you will be used to it. Minimize your non-school expenses. There is no better recipe for debt than to try to live like you have a full-time income when you only have a part-time income or, worse yet, no income at all.
- Work while you are studying. Yes, that is a hard prescription. School may take longer to complete and your life outside of work and school may be nonexistent, but it will keep your debt load down.
- Choose the lower-cost school. The school you attend is less important than the degree you get combined with your own personal talents and drive. Studies have concluded that it's the caliber of the student, not the school, that determines future earning power.[129]
- Apply for scholarships. Even for graduate school and non-degree programs, both scholarships and grants are available.

What about your kids? Most parents dream of sending their kids to college. If you haven't saved enough to pay for it though, it's important to help them plan for their education in a way that will minimize their outstanding debt. Here are some things to discuss with your college-bound kids:

- Tell your student how much you will be able to pay. This includes what you have saved and what you are willing to commit out of your income. Don't sacrifice your own retirement savings or take on your own debt to pay for college. Your kids will have time to recover from the expense. You won't.

- Outline options for raising the extra money. In addition to student loans and scholarships, your student may be able to raise some money through part-time or full-time work. Taking a gap year to work and save up for school is a reasonable approach.

- Provide context for the information. Estimate the kind of monthly salary your student might earn given her career interests. Payscale provides estimates in their College Salary Report at www.payscale.com/college-salary-report. It wouldn't hurt to also talk about average living expenses. Payscale also has a cost of living calculator at www.payscale. com/cost-of-living-calculator. Don't forget to show the impact of taxes. How much of her take-home pay will be left after student loan payments?

- Consider starting school at a community college. The average cost per year at public two-year colleges is only $3,435, assuming your student can stay at home while she attends. Some high schools allow students to attend community college and simultaneously earn college and high school credits with no tuition expenses.

For most, adding to your skills with an education—whether it's a technical degree, a bachelor's degree, or a graduate degree—will add to your income earning power. However, if you don't plan it well, you could wind up with a smaller lifestyle, not a better one. If you don't finish your education or decide you don't like the field, you may not earn more. If you compound that with loans to pay for your education, your income after loan payments could be lower than before you set out to get your degree.

Don't jump into school on a whim. It is an expensive and rigorous endeavor that is not to be taken lightly. Take out as little debt as possible. Understand what it will cost you before you borrow, and have a plan for repayment whether your education works out as you hope or not.

Getting Rid of Debt

Paying off your debt is a form of savings that is equally as good as, if not better than, socking money away in other accounts. If you have debt, you have negative savings. You are starting in a hole, and every dollar you save simply serves to offset a dollar of debt. So why not deal with that directly and fill in the hole?

Credit card debt can have interest rates of more than 15 percent. If you pay off your credit card, you get a guaranteed return of 15 percent on every dollar. You are unlikely to get such a high return in any investment, and it certainly would not be guaranteed.

Student loan interest rates can also be quite high. Government direct unsubsidized loans taken out before 2013 had an interest rate of 6.08 percent. Current undergraduate loans have a rate of 4.45 percent, and graduate loans have a rate of 6 percent.[130] Private loans have higher rates. If you were to pay these off, you would have a darned good rate of return for a guaranteed investment. Other loans, like car loans and mortgages, have lower

Tyrell

When Tyrell started college after eleven years in the workforce, he decided to pursue a career in health care. He hoped to become an osteopath. He got a degree in human physiology, racking up $54,000 in student loans in the process.

However, by the time he got his degree, he had become disenchanted with the osteopathy field. Instead he turned his sights on alternative medicine, and he decided to pursue acupuncture. Tuition for acupuncture school was $80,000, and Tyrell took out another $44,000 to cover living expenses. His total debt on graduation was $178,000, including the debt from his undergraduate degree.

In his estimation, this would have been manageable with a medical career. But he didn't recalculate when he decided to pursue alternative medicine. Acupuncture isn't a field where you can just go and find a job. Practitioners are generally self-employed, with less financial security than comes with a regular paycheck. Tyrell opened a practice with another acupuncturist.

Portland, Oregon, where Tyrell lives, has two acupuncture schools. Due to state licensing requirements, it is expensive and difficult to change states once you've gained your license in one. The result is an overpopulation of acupuncturists in the Portland area to the tune of about double what the market can support. Tyrell's business never took off.

When his partner could no longer pay his half of the bills and Tyrell could not afford the expenses of the office on his own, he closed his practice. After eighteen months, he hadn't made any money. Because his income was so low, he wasn't required to make payments on his debt. While he wasn't making payments, interest was growing, essentially causing him to borrow more with each passing month. His debt grew by another $18,000 to $196,000.

Tyrell took a job in tech support for a software company. The pay is good, and he has benefits. He's also teaching classes after work. He lives austerely. With cheap rent and minimal entertainment expenses, his goal is to have his loans paid off in five years.

In the meantime, he can't buy a house or a car, and even though he is nearly forty years old, saving for retirement will have to wait.

interest rates, but all have higher rates than comparable guaranteed investments.

Aside from the attractive guaranteed return of paying off your debt, eliminating your debt payments lowers your cost of living. That means you can afford to have a smaller emergency fund, and you have more money to save or do other things. Your financial flexibility will take a giant leap forward.

There are two very effective ways to pay down your debt: the **debt snowball** and the **debt avalanche**. Both methods involve paying only the minimum on all but one of your outstanding loan balances and then paying as much as you can afford on the one remaining loan. They differ in which loan you choose to focus on first.

With the debt snowball, you pick the loan with the smallest outstanding balance. On all other loans, you make the minimum

payment, but on your smallest balance loan, you make the largest payment you can afford to make. When that loan is paid off,
take all the money you have been paying on it and add it to the
minimum payment on the loan with the next smallest balance.
Keep it going across your loans, and eventually you will knock
off all your balances.

With the debt avalanche, you pick the loan with the highest
interest rate and focus your extra payments on it. This method
will have you paying less in interest. Which one ends up taking
a shorter time to eliminate your debt depends on the debt you
have. The table on the next page shows how each would play out
on some hypothetical debt obligations.

In this example, total minimum monthly payments are
$717.98. If you start by adding $100 per month to the retailer
card, taking it to $125 per month instead of $25, and progress to
each of the remaining obligations according to either the snowball or avalanche method, the debt will be paid off in about four
and a quarter years. If you would like to see how your own debt
snowball or avalanche would play out, check out the calculator provided by Financial Mentor at www.financialmentor.com
/calculator/debt-snowball-calculator.

The advantage of the snowball approach in this example is
that your required minimum payments decline faster. In just over
three years, your required payment is down to $305.16, less than
half where you started. If something unfortunate were to happen,
such as a job loss or illness that keeps you out of work, you would
have fewer fixed obligations to worry about. With the avalanche
method, it takes four years to get there. The advantage in the avalanche method is the total interest paid is $104 less.

Regardless of which one you choose, you can see they are both
effective at getting rid of your debt. Why are they so effective?

	Outstanding Balance	Interest Rate	Term	Minimum Payment
Retailer card	$325	18.0%	Revolving	$25.00
Credit card 1	$500	16.5%	Revolving	$25.00
Credit card 2	$4,500	12.5%	Revolving	$91.88
Car loan	$12,000	4.0%	60 months, 48 left	$270.95
Student loan	$18,000	6.8%	10 years, 6 left	
Total	$34,500			

Every dollar of extra payment you make above the minimum payment goes directly to pay down the principal balance of the loan. That leaves a smaller balance on which to pay interest. As the loan balance declines, the interest portion of the required payment also declines, meaning more of your money goes to reducing the loan balance. With each payment, your loan balance and interest owed decline faster.

There are a couple of exceptions in your quest to pay off debt. If you are eligible for the Public Service Loan Forgiveness program and your PAYE payment would be lower than the minimum

	Snowball		Avalanche	
	Months to Payoff	Total Interest Paid	Months to Payoff	Total Interest Paid
Retailer card	3	$9	3	$9
Credit card 1	7	$32	7	$32
Credit card 2	27	$770	27	$770
Car loan	38	$912	48	$1,006
Student loan	51	$3,357	52	$3,159
Total		$5,080		$4,976

standard payment, you could wind up paying less on your loan by seeing it through for the ten-year period rather than making extra payments.

Hold off on paying down your mortgage debt until you are on target with your monthly savings goals. Ultimately you will want to pay off your mortgage too, but the low interest rates and the fact that your home will increase in value over time makes saving and investing your money in other things more attractive.

Once you've eliminated your debt, you will have much more flexibility to save more money. Your emergency fund can be smaller, and you will have more money available to save for longer-term needs. This includes retirement savings and saving for all the other things you want to accomplish.

Vocabulary

Debt-to-income ratio: Your total debt payments divided by your income before tax. This ratio is used by mortgage lenders in conjunction with your credit score and the amount of your down payment to decide how much money to loan you to purchase a home.

Reverse mortgage: A type of mortgage available to those aged sixty-two and older. The mortgage lender loans you the money in a lump sum, as a line of credit, or as monthly payments. You do not need to make payments on your loan. The loan and accrued interest will be repaid out of the proceeds of the eventual sale of your home.

Revolving credit: A type of loan that doesn't have a fixed repayment date. As you pay off principal, it becomes available to borrow again. Loans that fall in this category are credit card debt and lines of credit.

Graduated payment plan: A student loan repayment plan where your payments start out low and gradually increase over the life of the loan. The initial payments may be less than the monthly interest, causing your loan to increase until the payments become large enough to cover the interest.

Pay As You Earn (PAYE) plan: A student loan repayment plan where your required payment is limited to 10 percent of your discretionary income. Discretionary income in this case is the difference between your family's income and 150 percent of the federal poverty level for a family of your size. After twenty or twenty-five years, depending on when you signed up for the program, the remaining balance of your loan will be forgiven. If it is forgiven and you are not part of the Public Service Loan Forgiveness program, the amount forgiven will be counted as taxable income.

Public Service Loan Forgiveness Program: For those working in qualifying public service, such as for the government or a nonprofit, if your student loan is not fully repaid in ten years, the balance will be forgiven. In this case, there are no tax consequences to the arrangement.

Debt snowball: A debt repayment strategy where you make only the minimum payment on all but the smallest of your loans. You pay as much as you can afford on the smallest loan until it is paid off. Once that loan is paid, move to the next smallest loan and make the same payment you were making on the two loans together until this loan is also paid off. Continue until all your debt is paid off.

Debt avalanche: A debt repayment strategy where you make only the minimum payment on all but the loan with the highest interest rate. You pay as much as you can afford on the loan with the highest interest rate until it is paid off. Once that loan is paid, move to the next-highest interest rate loan and make the same payment you were making on both loans until this loan is also paid off. Continue until all your debt is paid off.

Main Ideas

1. Debt can be minimized if you go at life with that intention. To the extent that you must take on debt, your debt payments should be no larger than 25 percent of your before-tax income.

2. Good debt is debt that comes with an asset, like a home or an education. Bad debt comes with neither. Even good debt can go bad if you take on too much or don't understand what you are signing up for.

3. Paying off debt is a form of saving with a guaranteed return equal to the interest rate on your loan.

4. Paying off debt increases your financial security and flexibility. Your emergency fund can be lower, and you have the room to save more toward your other financial goals.

5. When you pay more than the minimum required payment on a loan, all the extra payment goes toward principal. That reduces the amount of interest owed and increases the portion of future payments going to principal. That in turn further reduces the interest owed, creating a virtuous cycle that allows you to pay off the loan before its contractual term.

Chapter 8

When Things Don't Go According to Plan

LIFE CAN BE UNPREDICTABLE, AND DESPITE YOUR BEST-LAID plans, things can go wrong. You can't control everything, but you can control how you prepare and respond to the worst life throws at you. Setting financial goals and creating plans to work toward them will set you up to deal with adversity. Whatever progress you make will put you in a better position to deal with the things that come your way.

The preparation to realize your goals will allow you to quickly adapt to changing circumstances. The savings you will build because of your preparation will give you choices and some breathing room. It will give you time to recover, adapt to the new reality, and decide on new goals if necessary. If things go badly, you may not be unscathed, but you will be better off.

In Case of Emergency: Building an Emergency Fund

The importance of an emergency fund has been mentioned multiple times already, but it is so important that it is worth reiterating and going into more detail. In the 2012 National Financial Capabilities Study done by the FINRA Investor Education Foundation, it was reported that 60 percent of Americans do not have three months of living expenses set aside for a rainy day. Even high-income earners didn't have money set aside. Of those making more than $75,000 per year, 35 percent didn't have an emergency fund.[131]

Yet there is a good chance that most will need one at some point. In 2016, about one job was lost to mass layoffs for every four jobs that were created in the United States.[132] More than one in four of today's twenty-year-olds can expect to be out of work for at least a year because of a disabling condition before they reach the normal retirement age.[133] Between potential job losses and times when you can't work because you're sick or injured, there is a pretty high probability that you won't be able to bring home a paycheck at some point during your career.

For too many, the loss of a paycheck is the start of a financial disaster. The lower your savings, the more quickly your bills can't be paid. Like with any disaster, the better prepared you are ahead of time for the loss of your income, the better you will be able to weather the storm. Just as you would set aside food, water, and batteries for the possibility of a power outage, you must set aside money to tide you over if you lose your job or can't work due to an illness or injury.

Start by creating a disaster recovery plan for your expenses. Know ahead of time what expenses you could cut if you or your partner weren't able to bring in a paycheck. In chapter 5, you defined how you spend your money. With that information, you can more easily figure out what expenses you can and cannot cut. Not only will that reduce the size of the emergency fund that you need but it will save you the stress of deciding when you are already worried about the loss of your income.

The rule of thumb is to have three months of living expenses set aside in an emergency fund. While three months of living expenses is a good place to start, you will want to evaluate your own situation. It is harder to find work in some careers than others.

If yours is a two-income household, the minimum you need to set aside must cover the difference between your reduced monthly expenses and the lowest income in the relationship. The chance that you will both lose your job at the same time is lower than the chance either one of you will lose your job, unless you work in the same industry or company. You can get away with assuming you'll only lose one of your incomes. To be on the conservative side, you would assume you lost the highest income and had to live on the lower income. Of course, for one-income households, you'll have to be able to fully cover your mandatory monthly expenses.

Use the following worksheet to calculate your emergency fund needs. You may have different mandatory expenses, so add in any that aren't shown in the worksheet.

Monthly Income	Example	*You*
Total household income	$5,000	
Lowest income	$2,000	
Assumed income lost	$3,000	

Assume you cut out nonessential spending while you are out of work.

Mandatory Expenses	Example	*You*
Housing	$1,200	
Childcare	$600	
Insurance	$200	

Mandatory Expenses	Example	*You*
Debt	$600	
Groceries	$450	
Gas	$250	
Other	$0	
Total	**$3,300**	

Emergency Fund	Example	*You*
A. Mandatory expenses	$3,300	
B. Remaining income (the lowest income)	$2,000	
C. Monthly shortfall (A − B)	$1,300	
D. Minimum emergency fund (C × 3)	**$3,900**	

Your emergency fund is your first line of defense against financial devastation. If yours is adequate, you can avoid going into debt and protect your savings for your long-term goals. What could otherwise be a serious setback could instead be just a minor detour. Having an emergency fund needs to be your number-one financial goal.

Insuring Your Income: Disability Insurance

To guard against the loss of your income due to illness or injury, you have another tool available: **disability insurance.** Disability insurance provides income replacement if you are unable to work after an accident or illness. It comes in two forms: short-term disability and long-term disability. Short-term disability insurance covers absences of between 60 and 180 days and can pay as much as 80 percent of your gross salary.

Long-term disability insurance picks up where short-term disability leaves off and can provide benefits for years, depending on the policy and the nature of the disability. Long-term disability will typically replace about 60 percent of your salary. That would be a big help and would extend the life of your emergency fund while you are getting a grip on how long you'll be out of work.

You can buy private disability insurance either through your employer or through an agent. While the need for homeowner's, car, and even life insurance is well understood, few insure against the loss of their income due to a temporary or permanent disability. Yet what is more valuable than your ability to earn a living?

Many employers offer both forms of disability insurance. Often employees will be automatically enrolled in short-term disability coverage, frequently at no cost to the employee. However, long-term disability insurance is generally a voluntary benefit requiring the employee to pay for much of the premium. Many employees skip the coverage to save money. Fewer than one in three private-sector workers is covered by long-term disability insurance.[134]

In case you think you would be eligible for other support, such as workers' compensation insurance or Social Security Disability Insurance, think again. Only one in twenty disabling illnesses or accidents are work related, which means that nineteen in twenty would not be covered by workers' compensation insurance.

Social Security Disability Insurance, like the retirement benefit, is based on your average earnings. If you are our hypothetical thirty-five-year-old and making $60,000 per year, you could be eligible for as much as $1,800 per month[135] (the average benefit is $1,197[136]), which is about one-third of what you are currently making. Will you be able to live on that much less income?

If long-term disability insurance isn't available through your employer, you can buy an individual policy. You can expect to pay between 1 and 3 percent of your annual salary for coverage. If your employer offers the coverage, it will likely cost less, so just take it. Even at individual policy prices, the expense is well worth it, given what you can expect to lose if you do become disabled.

The longer you are out of work, the more likely it is you will have to make changes to your plans. Even the most thorough disaster recovery plan only goes so far. But an emergency fund and disability insurance can give you some breathing room while you make changes to your lifestyle to deal with a lower income.

Adapting to What Actually Happens

Sometimes stuff happens that you just couldn't see coming. Even if you have done all that you could to prepare for financial setbacks, sometimes it's not enough. You just need a new plan.

For a good number of people, the financial crisis and Great Recession of 2008 and 2009 were just such an event. Those just graduating from college or with a newly minted professional degree walked out into an economy that didn't have a place for them. And many of them had student loans to pay.

Jeanna had just graduated from law school at the time, and legal jobs were in short supply. Before starting law school, she made some very deliberate choices that reduced the impact of this situation. She had become very frugal to minimize the cost of her lifestyle while she was in school. She also worked part-time

Ben and Amanda

Ben and Amanda were looking forward to a comfortable income in retirement from Ben's government and Amanda's corporate pensions. They knew just how they wanted to spend their time. Ben volunteered with the Forest Service, educating hikers on wilderness safety. He loved the excuse to hike and meet new people, and he wanted to do more of it. Amanda was looking forward to traveling.

Unfortunately, over the years Ben's work changed for the worse. He felt ill-suited for the responsibilities he was given, and his managers weren't willing to reassign him. His performance was criticized, and Ben felt badgered and unheard. Eventually, when he couldn't face his job another day, he took early retirement.

Not only did he give up his full-time work paycheck, but because he hadn't put in enough time at his job, his pension was drastically lower than he had previously expected it would be. To make matters worse, for some federal employees pensions automatically decline once the beneficiary is eligible for Social Security. So Ben was forced to take Social Security early, at sixty-two, cutting his potential benefit by a quarter. Not only did the couple need to adjust to a lower current income but their retirement income was permanently curtailed as well.

It was stressful as the couple scrambled to adapt. Ben looked for work, but jobs were scarce. They evaluated their spending and made changes so they could live and continue to save for retirement on Amanda's salary alone. Amanda was afraid their retirement dreams were gone.

> Their efforts to adapt to their new world paid off. Eventually Ben did find new work, and the couple socked away more in savings. Ben fully retired after working in retail for a few years. By maximizing her 401(k) contributions and eliminating debt, Amanda built their savings to the point where she could retire as well, even a few years earlier than expected.

while going to school to cover living expenses. Therefore she only needed student loans to cover tuition, fees, and books.

She still graduated with about $90,000 in debt, which is on the low end for professional graduates. Even so, it was a staggering amount to her. It frightened her to have that hanging over her head.

When she couldn't find a job in her field, Jeanna took a non-legal job at an insurance company so she could make the required payments on her debt and keep it from growing. She kept her lifestyle frugal, paid down the loans quicker than scheduled, and saved for retirement. After a few years, she landed a position as a staff lawyer at the company where she worked. She fulfilled her dream, and her loans were paid off.

Jeanna made important choices and set limits that helped her stay on track financially despite the job market setback. She decided that graduating law school with a manageable amount of debt was important enough for her to commit to a very low-cost lifestyle. When legal jobs weren't available, she chose to temporarily take something different to avoid deferring her loans, and she maintained her low-cost lifestyle. That allowed her to eliminate her debt and save for the future.

Not all your plans will come to fruition as you envisioned. Sometimes they are delayed, and sometimes they are completely derailed. All you can do is take a step back and evaluate what you have and where you can go next. The preparation to achieve your original goals will go a long way in helping you down the path toward new ones.

Dealing with Divorce

Contrary to popular opinion, divorce rates in the United States are down, according to data from Justin Wolfers, a University of Michigan economist.[137] If current trends continue, two-thirds of marriages will never end in divorce. That is the good news.

The bad news is that for those relationships that do end in divorce the financial toll can be devastating. The average cost of a divorce trial can run between $15,000 and $30,000.[138] In some cities, the cost is much higher. But that is just the beginning. After the divorce, previously shared expenses are no longer shared. To maintain the same lifestyle after divorce as before will cost you about 30 percent more. Spousal and child support can severely limit your ability to save.

Money shouldn't keep you in a bad marriage, but thinking through the financial impact of a breakup ahead of time can help maintain your financial security after. Here are a few things to consider before making the break that can make life afterward a little less difficult.

Understand your financial situation before you start down the divorce path. If possible, clear joint debt before you divorce. At the very least, open new credit card accounts in your separate names and transfer the old balances between them. If you have car loans or other debt, separate those as well. Regardless of who is supposed to pay the debt according to the divorce agreement, creditors can pursue you on joint accounts if your former spouse doesn't pay.

If you own a house, it may be a better idea to sell it before the divorce than for one spouse to get it in the divorce. If you get the house, you may get less in financial assets, or you may have to buy your spouse out by refinancing. Either way, you'll have less income and won't have reduced your expenses. If you sell the house, the proceeds can be split and used for a down payment for each of you on a new home that will fit within your new smaller budget. If you agree to sell later, you may create an opportunity for further conflict.

When dividing assets, keep an eye on future tax consequences. Traditional IRAs and 401(k)s will generally be fully taxable upon withdrawal, while Roth and nonretirement accounts will not be. A dollar in a traditional IRA or 401(k) is worth less than the same dollar in a Roth or nonretirement account because of the tax bite. If you have both types of accounts, take the tax consequences into consideration when dividing them. Once the accounts are divided, make sure to update your beneficiaries.

Develop a post-divorce budget. While maintaining your life-style will cost 30 percent more, you're not likely to get a pay raise of that magnitude. Think of ways you can reduce your cost of living so that you can avoid going into debt and continue to work toward your future financial security.

The divorce is not the place to get your revenge. No one wins except the attorneys when you use the legal process to inflict pain. Regardless of how hurt you feel, take the emotion out of the divorce.

Consider it a business transaction. If you and your spouse can agree on how to divide your property, the cost of your uncontested divorce could be as little as $200, about 1 percent of the average contested divorce.

Divorce is painful and costly in so many ways. You have to establish a whole new life for yourself, and that means new hopes and dreams and financial goals. It's easy to leave off that last one, but it's a critical piece given how financially costly a divorce can be.

Mason married the love of his life, Natalie. They had two boys and settled into a lifestyle that allowed them to save for both an early retirement and college. But in 2008, Mason's life blew up. He went through a contentious divorce with Natalie. He won full custody of his sons, but Mason was required to pay Natalie nearly half of his income for five years.

With half of his income gone and two boys to raise, his early retirement plans were in jeopardy. But Mason didn't let the divorce derail him. He reduced his expenses as much as he could, cutting out extras like cable and eating out. He found that he could live and still save within his new lower income.

By the time the alimony payments ended, Mason had adjusted to a less expensive lifestyle. He did take advantage of the increased cash flow for a few luxuries, but he decided to save most of it. He paid off his mortgage, and with the boys finishing up high school, his goal of retiring early was in the bag.

Mason focused on his early retirement goal and managed the one thing that he knew he could control: his expenses. Knowing your financial situation, developing new savings goals, and creating a plan to get back on track while protecting yourself from future uncertainties will help you manage a divorce better and maintain your financial security after.

Life is uncertain. You can't tell when or if you'll experience a job loss or serious health issue. You can't change the economy, and not all relationships work out. Things happen that you just can't control. But you can control what you do about it.

We are so adaptable. We can still be happy even if our original goal doesn't pan out. But that doesn't mean having a goal and working toward it aren't worthwhile. In fact, the great uncertainty that life brings makes it all the more important. Yes, life may force you to change your plans. When it does, take stock of what you have and what you can make of it. Then make a new plan.

Vocabulary

Disability insurance: Insurance that will partially replace your salary if you are unable to work after an accident or illness. It comes in two forms: short-term and long-term. Short-term disability insurance covers absences of between 60 and 180 days and can pay as much as 80 percent of your gross salary. Long-term disability insurance picks up where short-term disability leaves off and can provide benefits for years, depending on the policy and the nature of the disability.

Main Ideas

1. Everyone needs to have money set aside to cover expenses for at least three months should they lose their job or be unable to work due to an injury or illness.
2. Disability insurance is just as or more important than property or life insurance. What could be more valuable than your ability to earn a living?
3. There is usually more than one way to achieve your goals and financial security.
4. Pay attention to what you can control: your expenses and how much you save.
5. When life gets in the way of your plans, make a new plan.

PART 3

Chapter 9

Where to Put Your Money

YOU HAVE MANY GOALS, BUT THERE ARE THREE FUNDAMENTAL savings goals that everyone needs to work toward. You need an emergency fund, you need to save so you can cover your expenses when you stop working for pay, and you need to eliminate debt.

Of course, there are other financial goals. Maybe a down payment for a house, college for the kids, a wedding, or a trip. Ideally you would work toward all your financial goals at once. Some, like retirement and college, require large amounts of savings, and you will need as much time as possible to fund those goals. However, if you can't swing that right away, you need to prioritize. Your priorities must balance your financial security, time, and opportunities for investment returns.

First Things First: Your Emergency Savings

Once you have incorporated all your expenses into your budget and you've freed up room for savings, your first priority is to establish an emergency fund. If you don't have enough flexibility right now to do more than one thing, do this first.

You should be able to cover at least three months of your nondiscretionary expenses from your emergency fund. A worksheet for figuring out how much you need can be found in chapter 8.

After you've built up to your target savings, you can move on to other financial goals. You may need to add to your emergency savings if your have-to expenses rise or if you need to tap your savings for the emergency it's there for. But for the most part, your emergency savings is a one-and-done kind of goal.

Your emergency savings need to be in something safe so the money will be there when you need it. Options include a savings account at your bank or credit union, a money market mutual fund available through most financial institutions, certificates of deposit at your bank or credit union, or a high-yield savings account through an online bank.

Savings accounts and money market mutual funds are very flexible, with no limits on deposits or withdrawals. Some money market funds will have minimum initial deposit requirements though. Certificates of deposit are accounts that require you to leave your money on deposit for a minimum period that can range from one month to several years. An early withdrawal can result in the loss of interest earned and a possible penalty, but you will get a higher interest rate for the inconvenience. High-yield savings accounts have some restrictions but are generally more flexible than certificates of deposit.

Savings accounts, certificates of deposit, and high-yield savings accounts are backed by FDIC insurance and are therefore guaranteed up to $250,000. Money market accounts don't have the same backing but have a long history of being a safe place for your money.

Unfortunately, safe places for your money don't pay much in interest. Even the name "high-yield savings account" is more of a euphemism than a real promise of high interest rates. The following table summarizes the various savings vehicles and their interest rates as of mid-2018. To see a comparison across financial institutions, visit www.depositaccounts.com.

	Savings Account	Money Market Account	Certificate of Deposit (1 Yr)	High-Yield Savings Account
Available at	Banks and credit unions	Widely available at financial institutions	Banks, credit unions, some brokerage firms	Online banks
Minimum deposit required	Not usually	Maybe	Yes	Maybe
Minimum holding period	None	None	Yes	Maybe
Limits on number of transactions	None	None	Yes	Maybe
Withdrawal penalties	None	None	Yes	None
Average interest earned in 1 year on $1,000[a] as of June 2018	$2.16	$18.50	$8.67	$16.00

a. Deposit Accounts home page, accessed June 30, 2018, https://www.depositaccounts.com/.

Related to your emergency fund, if you have a high-deductible health insurance policy, also known as a **consumer-driven healthcare plan (CDHP)**, you should also save enough to cover your plan deductible, which can range from a few thousand dollars to over $7,000 per individual in these types of plans.

Most CDHPs come with a **health savings account (HSA)** so you can save to cover some of your deductible. This is one of those future expenses you should be predicting as part of your budget. For 2018, you could contribute up to $3,450 per individual or $6,900 for a family pretax. The savings are yours and you are not required to spend them in the year contributed.[139]

The savings can grow over time if you don't use them, allowing you to build up to the full deductible and eventually the out-of-pocket maximum. Because the contributions are pretax, you will get an implicit discount equal to your tax rate for whatever medical bills you do pay with them. Your employer may even make part of the contribution for you.

Having emergency savings and being able to cover at least your health care plan deductible are your first line of defense against the risks of life. They will help keep you from going into debt if you experience the misfortune of losing your job or falling ill. The money needs to be in a safe place so it will be there for you when you need it. Once you've built up your safety net, your other goals can take priority.

The Power of the Match: Retirement Plan Savings

If your employer offers a 401(k) or other similar retirement savings plan with a **matching contribution**, your next priority is to contribute enough to get the full match. A matching contribution is a deposit to your retirement account made by your employer in a stated proportion to what you contribute. It's free money.

Financial Engines, an investment advisory firm focusing on offering advice to retirement plan participants, reported in a recent study that nine in ten employers who offer a plan also provide an employer match.[140] But one in four employees did not receive the full match because they didn't contribute enough themselves, missing out on an average of $1,336 annually.

The most common formula for a matching contribution is dollar for dollar up to 6 percent of an employee's pay. If you make $60,000 per year, 6 percent of your pay would be $3,600 per year. If you contribute that amount, your employer would contribute the same, doubling your money guaranteed. There is no better investment return available, and it has a powerful impact on the growth of your retirement savings.

If you are in your twenties, your savings plus a match like this would be just about all you would need for a secure retirement, assuming you could keep it going for your entire career. If you are later in life, you'll need to save more, but this boost from your job will be a big help. If your investment returns averaged 7 percent per year, with this employer match your account balance would grow to nearly $103,000 in just ten years. The chart on the next page shows your contribution, the employer match, and the balance attributable to market return. With the employer match and market return, you have almost tripled your money.

If you seem to have a balance in your company's 401(k) plan but you didn't sign up for the plan, don't assume that you are getting the maximum employer match. Many plans use automatic enrollment to get employees saving but start the contributions at a low level that doesn't necessarily maximize the match. While you are saving—which is a good thing—you'll still need to increase your contribution on your own to get the biggest matching contribution possible.

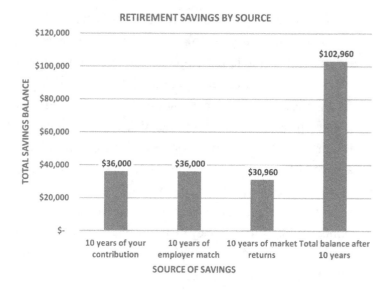

While the dollar-for-dollar match is the most common, there are unlimited possibilities. Speak with your employer about your plan so that you understand how to maximize their contribution to your savings. Once your emergency fund is in place, take full advantage of this valuable benefit.

To Roth or Not to Roth

About half of employers offering a retirement savings plan offer both a **traditional** plan and a **Roth** plan.[141] In a traditional plan, your contributions are taken from your pay before taxes. This makes it easier to save because the amount your paycheck is reduced by is less than the total you are saving by your combined state and local tax rate. Your savings will grow tax-free until you withdraw them, and that is when the government will get their share.

When you start withdrawing the money from your savings plan in retirement, your entire withdrawal will be taxed as income. If you have other sources of income at that time and you don't need to draw on your retirement savings account, you will still need to make a required minimum withdrawal from the account every year beginning six months after you turn seventy so the government can start getting some tax revenue on that money.

With a Roth plan, your contributions are after-tax. So if you contribute $3,600 over the course of a year, your paycheck will be lower by that amount. But Roth accounts have advantages on the back end. Your withdrawals in retirement are completely tax-free.

In addition, you are not required to take a minimum distribution, so your savings can continue to grow tax-free. Finally, withdrawals from your Roth account won't count as income in determining whether your Social Security benefits are taxable.[142] The following table compares traditional and Roth accounts with an example based on a single year's contribution for an equal reduction from your paycheck.

	Traditional	Roth
One year's contribution	$3,600	$2,700
Tax benefit on contribution	$900	$0
Deducted from pay	$2,700	$2,700
Balance after 20 years	$13,930	$10,448
Tax owed on withdrawal	$3,482	$0
After-tax withdrawal	$10,448	$10,448

Note: Assumes 25 percent state and local taxes and 7.0 percent average annualized return.

For the same reduction in your paycheck, you get a bigger contribution on the front end of your savings in a traditional account due to the tax benefit. If you assume tax rates don't change, the amount you can spend when you retire is the same regardless of the account, but you will pay more in total taxes from a traditional account.

If your tax rates are lower in retirement than they are now, you will have more money to spend with a traditional account. However, regardless of the eventual tax rate, the Roth account provides you with more flexibility when you are living on your savings.

Anyone whose employer offers one can contribute to an employer-sponsored Roth savings plan. There are no income limits as there are with a Roth IRA, which will be covered shortly. Your employer's contribution will still be made in the traditional plan, so you will wind up with some savings in a Roth account and some savings in a traditional account.

If you have been saving through a traditional retirement savings account at work, you can make your future contributions to a Roth account. Whether it's worthwhile to change your traditional savings into Roth savings is a trickier question, so it's worth getting some specific tax advice. If you convert your traditional retirement savings to a Roth account, the amount you convert will become taxable income in the year you make the change.

You can't predict what your taxes will be when you retire, but if you have done your job right and saved enough to support yourself, it's a good bet you'll be paying them. Having some savings that aren't subject to required withdrawals or taxes will be an advantage.

Fill the Hole: Pay Off Your Debt

Now that you have your emergency fund in place and you are taking full advantage of your employer's matching contribution to your retirement savings, the next step is to begin eliminating your debt. Every dollar of debt you have reduces your financial flexibility. Paying off your debt is a form of savings equally as good as any other form, and it will have the added bonus of freeing up more money for you to save later.

The following table shows average interest rates by type of loan.

	2018 Interest Rate	Notes
Credit cards	15.0%	
Personal loans	10.6%	
Car loans	4.75% and up	Depending on credit, term, and lender
Student loans[a]	4.4% to 8.5%	Depending on the program and when the loan was taken
30-year mortgages[b]	4.75%	

Source: Federal Reserve, "Consumer Credit—G.19."
a. Federal Student Aid, "Interest Rates and Fees."
b. BankRate.com, "Current Mortgage Rates."

With any of these loans, for every dollar of principal you pay off, you are earning a guaranteed return equal to the interest rate on the loan. Pay down your credit card and get a guaranteed return of 15 percent. There is no other investment that pays a guaranteed return that high. For that matter, there is no guaranteed investment that has a return as high as any of these interest rates in today's low-interest-rate world.

Debt is essentially negative savings. As long as you have debt outstanding, you continue to pay someone else for the use of their money. Debt means that you pay more for what you buy—substantially more in the case of things purchased with a credit card.

Debt payments are not optional. You have to make them regardless of whether you are working. So if you have debt, you need to have a larger emergency fund to cover the payments in the event you lose your income temporarily. For your financial security, you need to eliminate debt. Two methods for eliminating debt were provided in chapter 7.

If you have a mortgage, the interest rate is low enough that paying it off should not come before your other long-term savings goals like retirement. You need as much time as possible to build up the savings you will live on when you stop working for pay. Since you will likely earn a much higher return on your retirement savings than the interest rate on your mortgage, put your energy and extra money toward that instead.

If you can meet your savings goals and pay down your debt at the same time, then do both. But getting rid of your debt is an important goal, and if your debt load is currently keeping you from saving, getting rid of it needs to be a priority.

More Retirement Savings

Once you have eliminated your nonmortgage debt, if you aren't meeting your monthly target retirement savings, increase your contributions to your employer-sponsored retirement savings plan. As of 2018, you can save up to $18,500 per year in your plan. If you are fifty or older, you can save $24,500 per year.

Employer-sponsored plans have received some bad press in the past few years, and the concerns voiced may give you pause about saving more there. However, for most people, your employer's retirement savings plan is a great way to save. They offer higher savings limits than other retirement savings accounts and are cost-effective. The fact that most plans are cost-effective makes the criticism ironic.

The criticism revolves around fees. Every cent of fees you pay is investment earnings you don't get to keep, and high fees do take a toll on your savings. In a company-sponsored retirement plan, there are four broad categories of fees. There are the fees associated with making the plan work, called administrative fees. Some plans also charge transaction fees and fees for special services. Finally there are the investment expenses collected by the investment companies for managing the investment options.

The first set of fees is out of your hands. Your company se-lected the plan and hopefully made the best deal possible. For large plans, administrative fees make up only a small portion of total fees. In small plans, on average they represent 15 percent of total fees. Whether your plan is large or small, investment ex-penses are your biggest expense.[143]

Investment expenses are required to be disclosed to partic-ipants. You will generally find the expenses on the information page for the investment option. You are looking for the **expense ratio**, which is the annual expenses of running the fund divided by the total market value of all the investments in the fund. You may find a variety of expense ratios disclosed, but for apples-to-apples comparisons, focus on the annual gross expense ratio, which is calculated the same way for all funds.

Fund expenses are embedded in the price of the fund. You won't see them come out of your account because they are taken out of the share value of the fund. They include what is paid to the investment manager; expenses to market the fund (called

12b-1 fees); and trading, regulatory, and record-keeping expenses. The higher these expenses are, the higher the expense ratio will be.

Participants in 401(k) plans generally have options that are lower cost than outside the plan. In 2015, the average expense ratio for a fund investing in equities (shares of companies' stock) was 1.31 percent. The average expense ratio on the same type of fund in 401(k) plans was only 0.53 percent. Only 11 percent of 401(k) plan assets were invested in equity mutual funds with an expense ratio higher than 1 percent.[144]

For a few, the employer-sponsored plan is a bad deal. About 12 percent of 401(k) assets were invested in funds with some variety of sales charge that could boost the investment expenses beyond a reasonable level.[145] However, most plans make low-cost funds available, even if other options are expensive.

Chances are your employer-sponsored retirement savings plan is a cost-effective way to save for retirement, and the saving limits are higher than the limits on other tax-advantaged accounts. After you have eliminated your high-cost debt, return to your retirement plan and increase your contribution.

Education and Nonprofit: A Special Case

People who work for public schools, health care workers, and others who work for charitable organizations have a version of the employer sponsored retirement savings plan called the **403(b)**.

In some respects, it is very much like the 401(k) plan. Contributions are tax-exempt as are investment earnings. There is often a Roth option available, and the saving limits are the same as the 401(k). Regulations that came out in 2006 encouraged plan sponsors to move their plans in the direction of 401(k) plans, and in some cases 403(b) plans are indistinguishable from a 401(k) plan.

However, some 403(b) plans offer a long list of providers, and participants must figure out which providers are best for them. If that sounds like your plan, here are a couple of things to watch out for.

First, be cautious with insurance company providers. Not all insurance company offerings are bad, but too many are in this arena. They can have hefty fees attached to benefits that most don't need in their retirement savings vehicle, and you may be subject to a surrender charge period. If you want to move your investments to a different provider, you must wait until the surrender period is up or face a penalty. Surrender periods can be several years long.

Mutual fund providers are easier to navigate because their fees are more readily available. But be wary of mutual fund providers offering funds with sales charges. Some providers in 403(b) plans offer funds that scrape a commission off every contribution. Every deposit you make will have a deduction taken to pay some salesperson you may never have met. These funds are called Class A shares.

Many retirement plans offer Class A shares, but most waive the commission. If they do waive the commission, there will be a notation that the shares are "load-waived." Focus on providers that offer load-waived or other noncommissioned shares. Reject the provider if the funds are not load-waived shares.

Find out if your employer offers a **457 plan**. Yes, yet another work-related plan. These plans can have multiple providers but tend to be simpler than 403(b) plans. If you have both, you have a unique advantage that other retirement plan participants do not. You can make the maximum contribution to both your 457 plan and your 403(b) plan. If your 457 plan's investments are lower cost, invest there first.

More to Saving Than Work

You may be among the 42 percent of Americans who do not have access to a retirement plan at work, or you may be a business owner yourself.[146] Perhaps you are late to the saving game, you have a high income, or you want to retire early. In these cases, you may not be able to save enough in your work-related retirement plan to meet your savings goals. But there are options beyond an employer-sponsored retirement plan.

There are ways to save that have been around for a long time and have all the same tax advantages of a company retirement plan. If you don't have a plan at work or you have maxed out your employer-sponsored savings plan, the good old individual retirement account (IRA) is still there for you. The contribution limits are lower, but the earnings grow without being taxed as they would in a 401(k). The table on the next page shows the features of the Roth and traditional IRA accounts for 2018.

The Roth IRA has the exact same advantages relative to a traditional IRA as the Roth 401(k) has relative to a traditional 401(k), which was shown earlier in this chapter. If your income is too high to allow you to save directly to a Roth IRA, and you don't have any savings in a traditional IRA, with an extra step you can still have all those advantages.

The IRS allows you to contribute to a traditional IRA and then immediately convert it to a Roth IRA, creating what is known as a "backdoor Roth." With an immediate conversion, there are no earnings to tax, so the conversion is tax-free.

However, be careful. If you already have traditional IRA savings due to previous 401(k) rollovers or your past contributions, this backdoor Roth contribution probably won't work for you. That is because the IRS lumps all your traditional IRA holdings

	Roth IRA	Traditional IRA
2018 contribution limits	$5,500	$5,500
2018 over 50 catch-up contribution limit	$6,500	$6,500
Tax treatment contributions	Contributions are made after-tax.	Contributions are tax-deductible if you don't have a work-related retirement plan and your income is less than $73,000 for singles and $101,000 if married; otherwise, after-tax.
Tax treatment withdrawals	Withdrawals after age 59.5 are tax-exempt. Contributions can be withdrawn prior to age 59.5 without penalty, but earnings are taxed and subject to a 10% penalty.	Withdrawals after age 59.5 are taxed as ordinary income. Withdrawals prior to age 59.5 are taxed and incur a 10% penalty. Withdrawals of contributions made after-tax are tax-exempt.
Eligibility	Anyone with an adjusted gross income less than $120,000 for singles and $189,000 if married	Anyone

	Roth IRA	Traditional IRA
Required minimum distribution	None	Proportion of your account each year after age 70.5

together and will tax your current contribution according to the proportion of the balance that hasn't already been taxed.

Roth and traditional IRA accounts can be opened at any financial institution. Discount brokerage firms like Charles Schwab and E-Trade offer low transaction fees and access to mutual funds from a broad array of companies as well as low-cost exchange-traded funds, corporate stocks, and government and corporate bonds. There will be more on investments in chapters 10 and 11.

You can also invest directly with a mutual fund company and enjoy no transaction fees when you invest in their funds. Most fund companies also have a brokerage service available that allows you to buy other companies' mutual funds or stocks and bonds for a fee.

For Business Owners

If you are a business owner, you can start out with a Roth or traditional IRA, but as your ability to save grows, there are options available to you with higher contribution limits. The Savings Incentive Match Plan for Employees of Small Employers, or **SIMPLE IRA**, the Simplified Employee Pension (**SEP-IRA**), and the **Solo 401(k)** have several advantages.

They have higher contribution limits than IRAs and in some cases higher limits than 401(k)s. They are easy to set up and do not have the reporting requirements of typical employer-sponsored retirement plans. Also, in all cases participants are responsible for their own investment decisions. Most financial institutions can easily accommodate these accounts.

	SIMPLE IRA	Simplified Employee Pension (SEP-IRA)	Solo 401(k)
2018 contribution limits	$12,500 for employer and employee contributions. If you are one and the same, $25,000.	The smaller of $53,000 or 25% of your income.	$18,500 for employee and 25% of income for employer. Combined contributions as employer and employee of $55,000.
Required contributions	Minimum 2% or matching 3% of employee pay. Must contribute the same percentage of pay to employee accounts as you do your own. Employees can elect to contribute.	Must contribute the same percentage of pay to all employee accounts. Amount can vary from year to year. Only the employer contributes.	None

	SIMPLE IRA	Simplified Employee Pension (SEP-IRA)	Solo 401(k)
Tax treatment contributions	Pretax	Pretax	Pretax for traditional and after-tax for Roth
Tax treatment withdrawals	Fully taxable	Fully taxable	Taxable if traditional, tax-exempt if Roth
Eligibility	Any small business— usually with 100 or fewer employees	Any business	Business owners with no employees or owner and spouse
Required minimum distribution	Proportion of your account each year after age 70.5	Proportion of your account each year after age 70.5	Proportion of your account each year after age 70.5 if traditional, none if Roth

Early Retirement or High Incomes

For those who are on the early retirement track or who have high incomes, even the limits associated with these retirement accounts may be too constraining. If you have maxed out all your tax-advantaged savings options and still need to save more to meet your financial goals, your only remaining option is to go taxable.

In a taxable account, your earnings are taxed every year as part of your income. When you sell an investment at a profit, you will pay a capital gains tax as well, though investment losses and transaction expenses are tax-deductible.

Don't let the constraints of your work-related retirement plan—or lack of a plan—keep you from saving what you need to for retirement. Individual retirement accounts have been around for a long time. You can open one at just about any financial institution. And you can always save the old-fashioned way in a taxable account.

College Savings

College savings, like retirement, requires time because the amounts are so large. It makes sense to start as early as you can. But unlike you and your retirement, your kids will have more time to recover if their education isn't fully paid for by you. Only once you are reaching your current monthly savings goals for retirement should you consider saving for college as well.

You can save for college with a tax-advantaged account too. Many states offer **529 college savings plans**. In these accounts, the earnings grow tax-free, and withdrawals for qualified educational purposes are tax-free as well. You can also get a state tax deduction for your contribution in thirty-four states.[147] You can actually save in any state's plan, but if you don't live in the same state as the plan, you won't get the tax deduction.

Money in a 529 savings plan can be used at any accredited college or university in the United States and at some foreign institutions as well. With the 2018 tax reform, it can now also be used for private K–12 expenses too. There are no income limits, age limits, or annual contribution limits. Total lifetime contributions vary by state plan but range from $235,000 to $500,000.

You can open a 529 plan account through your state, the mutual fund company operating the plan, or through a financial adviser. Some states offer 529 prepaid plans too. These plans are designed to fund education at in-state public schools. The savings can be transferred to other institutions, but you may not get the full value. The 529 savings plan offers more flexibility.

In addition, you can save for college in a **Coverdell Education Savings Account**. These accounts are not state specific, and you can open one with any financial institution. The contribution limit is $2,000 per year, and earnings grow tax-free until withdrawn. Contributions are not tax-deductible, but withdrawals are tax-free for qualified educational expenses. The main benefit of the Coverdell account is that it allows you to invest in anything your financial institution offers. The 529 plan investment options are limited by what the fund company operating the plan offers.

If your child does not use the savings in these accounts, you can transfer the savings to another family member or use them yourself. If the savings are withdrawn but not used for education, you will pay taxes on the earnings at your current tax rate plus a 10 percent penalty. That sounds bad, but if your savings have grown, you will still get more back than you put in because the taxes and penalty are assessed on the earnings.

On the House

Now that your savings are on track, it's time to think about paying down your mortgage. Even at low interest rates, it's worth paying off your home early. Just as with any form of debt, the interest on your mortgage increases the cost of owning a home. For most it's not possible to buy a home without a loan, but getting rid of your loan early can save you an enormous amount of money.

Say that you have a thirty-year mortgage of $100,000 at an interest rate of 4 percent. If you make the normal monthly payments, you will pay $71,867 in interest over the life of the loan. You will have paid almost three-quarters more than the original loan balance for your home.

If you were to double your payment, you could have your home paid off in less than eleven years. Your interest paid would be only $23,206. That is a savings of nearly $48,661. Every dollar of extra payment goes to the principal of the loan and reduces the overall interest paid. Even committing small amounts to paying down the loan can allow you to pay it off quicker and save on interest.

Eliminating your mortgage before you stop working for pay makes a big difference. With no mortgage payments, your draw on your savings will be smaller, making that pool of money last longer. If your savings suffer from an investment market downturn, you will be better able to weather it because your overall expenses will be lower.

Compare two women, Valerie and Jocelyn. Both are single and recently retired. Valerie has a pension from her government job and a bit of savings, while Jocelyn has retirement savings and Social Security. Both women will have about the same amount to live on, around $4,000 per month.

Valerie, due to a recent divorce, will have to take on a mortgage of around $100,000. Her payments will be at least $477 per month excluding taxes and insurance. With the new mortgage payment, Valerie's expenses will consume all her income. As other expenses increase with inflation, Valerie may find her budget pinched and need to find ways to cut back on her lifestyle.

Jocelyn's home is paid off. She estimates her normal expenses will be less than she will receive from Social Security alone. That leaves her plenty of room for home improvements, vacations, and other extras with the income from her savings. She has much more financial flexibility. Her cost of living is low and has plenty of room to grow if inflation forces it up. Jocelyn is much more financially secure than Valerie.

If you have other high-cost debt, and if you need to be saving more in your retirement accounts, paying down your mortgage should be the last thing on your list. However, if you are meeting your other savings goals, paying off your mortgage early will dramatically reduce your cost of housing and increase your flexibility. It is particularly important to have your mortgage paid off before you stop bringing home a paycheck. The lower your monthly expenses, the greater your financial security.

Keep It Simple

These days, it's easy to grow the number of your investment accounts. According to The Balance, a career advice website, the average person will change jobs twelve times during their career.[148] That means potentially twelve different 401(k) accounts if you're a good saver. That's in addition to the variety of different accounts you could have outside of your 401(k).

You may have IRAs, college 529 plans, and taxable savings. Maybe your neighbor or brother-in-law sells investments, so you opened accounts with him. As long as you're saving, how can it be bad?

When it comes to your money, keeping things simple is your best approach. Consider choosing a single mutual fund company or discount brokerage firm to hold your savings outside your company-sponsored retirement plan. If you change jobs, roll your 401(k) savings into either your new employer's retirement plan or into an individual retirement account at your fund company or brokerage firm. A bonus benefit to consolidating

Gary and Brenda

Gary and Brenda were good savers. They stashed money away every chance they got, and they ended up with more accounts than they could keep track of.

When they sold their Silicon Valley home for a profit, a financial adviser invested some of the money in a variable annuity. They had money in college 529 plans for their three daughters. They each had retirement plans through work: Gary had a 401(k) plan, and Brenda had accounts with three different providers through her 403(b) plan. They also had IRAs with a mutual fund company and taxable savings in yet another financial institution.

Gary and Brenda had so many accounts they didn't even know how much money they had in savings. It was an effort to find all the statements. Some were dated, and not all the accounts had online access. They certainly did not know how the money was invested nor how much they were paying in fees. Once all the information was in front of them, they realized their investments were too aggressive for their age, and they were paying as much as 4.5 percent per year in fees on one account.

It wasn't going to be easy to simplify. Annuities can have long surrender charge periods, making it costly to get out of the contract within that period. The investments in the taxable accounts would incur capital gains taxes if they were sold in favor of consolidation and lower-cost investments. And of course, the employer retirement accounts and the 529 plans had to stay where they were.

While the taxable accounts couldn't be sold without taking a hit, most mutual fund companies have brokerage services that will take an in-kind transfer. That means the investments could be transferred to the same fund company that was holding the IRA accounts without any tax implications.

With their new awareness, Gary and Brenda could keep an eye on when the surrender period was up on the variable annuity. Though some taxes would be incurred on the earnings of that investment, the high costs associated with it made it worthwhile to try to transfer the money to lower-cost investments. Brenda could do the same with her 403(b) investments.

For Gary and Brenda, the biggest obstacle to meeting their financial goals was that they couldn't keep track of what they had. Consolidating as much as possible in one institution, even if it took some time, would help them monitor and manage their savings better.

your accounts with one financial institution is that, as your savings grow across your accounts, you may get additional or free services too.

Having as much of your savings in one place as possible will make it easier for you to manage your investments. As you approach retirement, it's important that your investments become more conservative so your money will be there for you when you need to spend it. Consolidating your investments in one place will allow you to see how your money is invested more easily and reduce the number of transactions you need to make.

Our lives are complicated enough. There isn't any need to add complexity with multiple investment accounts. Keeping as many of your accounts as you can in a single location will go a long way toward simplifying your financial life.

You may find it difficult to save for all your financial goals at once. Prioritize the goals that will keep you financially secure and those that will take the longest and most money to fulfill. As you knock off your shorter-term goals and pay off your debt, you will have more money to save for your other goals. Over time, your income will grow, and as long as your expenses don't grow to match, you will be able to save for all you want to accomplish.

Vocabulary

Consumer-driven healthcare plan (CDHP): Health care plans with lower monthly premiums but high deductibles. Most health care, other than wellness exams, must be paid out of pocket until the deductible is met.

Health savings account (HSA): A savings account made available with most CDHPs that allows you to set aside money for health care expenses pretax.

Matching contribution: A deposit to your retirement savings account made by your employer in a stated proportion to what you have contributed.

Traditional 401(k)/IRA: Retirement savings accounts where contributions are made pretax. Earnings on contributions grow tax-free until withdrawn. Withdrawals are fully taxable. After you turn seventy and a half, you must take and pay taxes on required minimum distributions from your account.

Roth 401(k)/Roth IRA: Retirement savings accounts where contributions are made after-tax. Earnings on contributions grow tax-free, and withdrawals after age fifty-nine and a half are tax-exempt.

Expense ratio: The annual expenses of running a mutual fund divided by the total market value of all the investments in the fund. The annual gross expense ratio is calculated the same way across all mutual funds and is the best one for comparing investment expenses.

403(b)/457 plans: Retirement savings accounts for nonprofit and government employees. The employer may make Roth versions available.

SIMPLE IRA/SEP-IRA: Retirement savings accounts designed primarily for small businesses, though any size business can use a SEP-IRA. With the SIMPLE IRA, the employer must provide a match for employees' contributions. With a SEP, only the employer contributes.

Solo 401(k): Retirement savings accounts for sole proprietors and their spouses. There are no contribution requirements, but the combined employer and employee (one and the same person in this case) contribution maximum is $55,000, with a standard employee contribution of $18,500 and up to 25 percent of income for the employer contribution. Solo 401(k)s can be opened as either traditional or Roth accounts.

College 529 plan: A tax-advantaged college savings plan. Contributions in thirty-four states are tax-deductible for state tax purposes up to a limit. You can save in any state's 529 plan. Earnings on savings grow tax-free, and withdrawals for educational purposes are tax-exempt.

Coverdell Education Savings Account: A college savings alternative that is not state specific. Money invested grows tax-free and can be invested in anything the financial institution has to offer. The annual savings limit is $2,000.

Main Ideas

1. Your top three savings priorities are funding emergency savings, contributing enough to your company retirement savings plan to get the full company match, and paying off your debt other than your mortgage.
2. While traditional retirement savings accounts have the up-front advantage of offering a tax deduction for your contribution, the tax-exempt withdrawal feature and additional flexibility can make Roth accounts a better option.
3. Saving for college is one of those goals that will take a long time. If you are saving enough to reach your retirement savings goals, start saving for college as soon as you can. But if you can't save enough for yourself, put saving for college off. Your kids will have more time to recover from the expense than you will have to save for your own future.
4. Paying off your mortgage should not be your top priority, but paying it off early significantly reduces the cost of your housing. It is especially important to have your mortgage paid off before you retire.
5. Keep your financial life simple by holding as many of your accounts as possible with the same financial institution.

Chapter 10

Introduction to Investing

SAVING ENOUGH IS THE MOST IMPORTANT PART OF CREATING a secure financial future. However, to get the most out of your savings, you will also need to invest it well. Regardless of age, education, or experience, many people don't know, are confused, or flat out have the wrong idea about the investment markets. It is understandable given the wide variety of advice you see in the media. There are so many different ideas because there is no one perfect way to invest.

In this chapter, you will learn some foundational terms and concepts to help you understand different investments and strategies. It is meant to help you differentiate among the investment options you see in your company-sponsored retirement plan and what is available through other financial institutions and advisers. It will also help you ask critical questions when someone is offering you advice or investment products. In chapter 11, you will learn easy ways to have your investments managed for you, but here you will learn what you are getting when you do.

The Three Investment Categories

Aside from cash and the variety of safe ways there are to hold your money outlined in the previous chapter, there are three other big investment categories. You can invest in them directly, or you can invest indirectly through what are essentially containers for these investment categories (more on this later). The three categories are stocks, bonds, and hard assets.

Stocks: Stocks are also known as equities. When you invest in stock, you own a small piece of a company. As an owner you share in the company's earnings with other owners. Your earnings may be sent to you in the form of a dividend, or the company might reinvest them in the business. Often it is a combination of the two.

Growth in earnings and dividends drives the long-term value of the shares you own, though many things influence the daily prices of stock in a publicly traded company. Publicly traded means the company's shares are traded on a stock exchange. Because future earnings are uncertain, stocks are risky investments.

Bonds: Bonds are also known as fixed income. When you invest in a bond, you own a piece of a loan made to a company or government. There are even bonds that bundle together credit card, auto, and mortgage loans to individuals, known as asset- or mortgage-backed securities. As the owner of a bond, you are entitled to interest and the return of principal, which is your piece of the amount loaned.

The daily value of a bond is driven by changes in interest rates, changes in the credit worthiness of the issuer, and the time remaining until the loan must be paid back. But if you hold the bond to maturity—when it must be paid back—you will simply get the interest and principal. Because the interest and principal payments are contractual obligations, bonds are less risky than stocks.

Hard assets: Hard assets are things you can touch, like precious metals, agricultural products, oil and gas, or real estate. The value of most hard assets is driven by supply and demand. They have no intrinsic ability to generate earnings. Real estate is the exception, as it can also generate income through rent. Supply and demand is unpredictable, so hard assets are also risky investments.

Within each of these broad categories is a host of subcategories. They include US and international stocks in large, mid-, or small sizes; US and international corporate and government bonds; and many more. There are thousands of companies and bond issues as well as many opportunities to hold hard assets.

Stocks

Stocks in publicly traded companies trade on stock exchanges and have publicly posted prices throughout the trading day. You can buy stock in small numbers of shares, though different financial institutions may require a minimum investment. While you don't need much money to buy a single company's stock, to create a well-rounded portfolio takes a substantial investment.

Stock in a single company is among the riskiest investments you can hold. The value can change dramatically over both short and long time periods. Owning several stocks helps with the single-company risk. As one company's business struggles, another may boom, offsetting the impact of the poor performer.

There have been a number of studies regarding how many stocks you need to own for a diversified portfolio. To offset the bulk of individual company risk, conventional wisdom suggests you should hold between twenty and forty companies' stock, assuming the companies are in different businesses.[149]

Bonds

Bonds are demarcated by credit worthiness and the term of the loan. Both drive the interest rate bonds pay as well as how much the price fluctuates between when it is issued and when it matures. Issuers with good credit are highly likely to pay what they owe but pay lower interest. Low-credit issuers pay higher interest, but there is a higher probability that they won't pay what they owe at some point.

The term of the loan also drives the interest paid on the bond. Longer-term bonds usually pay higher interest than shorter-term bonds. The daily valuations of longer-term bonds also fluctuate more than short-term bonds.

A typical bond investment strategy is called a bond ladder. This is a series of bonds with maturities in each year going forward for the time you choose. The interest payments and the payments at maturity together provide a flow of cash that is reasonably assured without your having to do anything after the initial purchase. A bond ladder is a good way to manage your withdrawals from your savings in retirement.

Hard Assets

Stocks and bonds are the meat and potatoes of a sound investment strategy. Hard assets are like the pepper. You don't need any at all, and if you do want to use them, they should be used sparingly.

Hard assets have grown in popularity since the financial crisis. They perform differently from the traditional equity markets, so they do offer diversification. However, it is important to have the right expectations. Different is not necessarily better. There will be times when they help your portfolio perform better than the more traditional investments, and there will be times when they drag your portfolio return down.

The same is true of bonds and cash. They behave differently from stocks. However, they are less risky than hard assets. You won't get the same risk reduction benefits from hard assets due to how risky they are on their own.

Creating your own portfolio from direct investments in stocks, bonds, and hard assets takes a great deal of time and effort. While you may save the cost of an investment manager, you are not likely to do as well as one. After all, they spend all day every day selecting investments and have far more resources for doing research. You, being employed elsewhere full-time, will devote far less time to managing your investments.

Instead you can own all these investments indirectly in professionally managed portfolios. Investment products that allow you to invest indirectly were designed to make owning investments easier for small investors.

Containers: Mutual Funds, ETFs, Insurance Products

One of the most widely available investments is the mutual fund. Mutual funds are **pooled investments** where an investment manager "pools," or combines, money from many people to buy a portfolio of investments that are shared by all those individuals. If a manager invests in thirty companies, all the investors in the fund own a portion of all thirty companies in the proportion that the manager has bought them.

With pooled investments, with one exception (ETFs, which you'll learn about shortly), there is a single price each day, called a unit price or net asset value. The price is calculated daily at the end of the day, based on the end-of-day value of the investments owned by the fund.

Mutual funds are the most prominent form of pooled investment vehicles. There was $16.3 trillion invested in mutual funds at the end of 2016. Other types include exchange-traded funds (ETFs), closed-end funds, and unit investment trusts (UITs). However, they represent a smaller share of the market. All in, there was over $19 trillion invested in pooled investments at that time.[150]

Mutual funds, as well as the other pooled investments, are classified by the way in which they invest your money. Funds can hold any kind of investments. However, funds that invest in equities represent the largest share of the market. As of 2016, about half of mutual fund assets and three-quarters of ETF assets were invested in stocks.[151]

Most funds focus on a particular niche of the investment market. These include large company stocks, like those that make up the S&P 500; small company stocks, many of which you may have never heard named; international company stocks; bonds; and a variety of other investments. Morningstar, a mutual fund analytics firm, classifies mutual funds into well over a hundred different categories.[152]

Funds may be **actively managed** or **passively managed**. Actively managed means the investment manager tries to perform better than a market index. An **index** is a fixed list of investments such as the S&P 500, which holds the five hundred largest company stocks in the United States, or the Dow Jones Industrial Average, which holds thirty industrial companies. There are hundreds of indices that slice and dice the investment market every which way you could imagine.

Passively managed means the investment manager replicates the returns of the index. Passively managed funds are commonly known as **index funds**. With an index fund, you are assured you will get returns in line with the index minus fund expenses.

With an actively managed fund, your returns may be higher or lower than the index. Actively managed mutual funds are generally more expensive than passively managed funds. The costs to attempt to beat an index, from additional staff and data to additional transactions, are higher than to manage a fund passively.

Fund expenses include the fee that is paid to the investment manager, a fee that is paid to the financial institution that holds the investments and calculates the unit price on the portfolio, administrative fees, and expenses to sell the fund to investors. Expenses are deducted from the investment values to arrive at the net asset value of the fund, meaning the price of the fund is already reduced by the cost to run it. Studies have shown that lower expenses are linked with higher performance.[153]

Fund companies often offer the same fund with multiple share classes. The share classes have different expenses and are sold to different investors. For example, Vanguard offers an S&P 500 index fund in two share classes.[154] The following table compares them. It is more cost-effective for mutual fund companies to have fewer large accounts, and they pass the savings on to their larger investors. Company-sponsored retirement plans often have access to lower-cost share classes.

	Investor Share Class	Admiral Share Class
Minimum investment	$3,000	$10,000
Fund expenses	0.14%	0.04%
Annual expenses on $1,000	$1.40	$0.40

Most people encounter mutual funds in their employer-sponsored retirement plan, but there are other ways to invest in them. Outside of your retirement plan, mutual funds are offered through stock brokerage firms, both full service (Merrill

Lynch, Morgan Stanley, etc.) and discount firms (Charles Schwab, E-Trade, etc.), banks, and directly from the mutual fund company.

In addition to the internal fund expenses, you may also pay a commission to buy and sell your mutual fund if you hold your investments through a brokerage firm or bank. However, brokerage firms often offer "no transaction fee" (NTF) funds; the brokerage firm is paid by the fund company instead of you.

These NTF funds generally have higher expenses than the transaction fee funds, but if your balance is small, they still may be more economical. If you buy your fund directly from the company that issues it, there is no transaction charge.

Exchange-Traded Funds (ETFs)

Exchange-traded funds (ETFs) are similar to mutual funds with one big exception: rather than being priced at the end of the day, they are traded on the stock market exchanges and priced by the market throughout the day. Most ETFs are index funds, and their values track the market indices they mimic.

ETFs have three advantages to investors over mutual funds. ETF expenses may be lower than similar mutual fund expenses for investors with small balances. For example, the Vanguard S&P 500 ETF has an expense ratio of 0.04 percent compared to the 0.14 percent on the investor share class.[155] Not all ETFs are less expensive than comparable mutual funds, but many are.

Another benefit for small investors who own their investments through brokerage firms, like Charles Schwab, is lower transaction costs. ETFs trade like stocks and have the same transaction costs. To buy an ETF through Charles Schwab, you will pay about five dollars per trade. Low-cost index mutual funds often don't provide any compensation to brokerage firms, so the transaction costs to buy them can be quite high. To buy or sell the

Vanguard Index 500 fund through Charles Schwab, for example, could cost you as much as seventy-six dollars per transaction.[156]

For taxable investments, outside your retirement accounts, ETFs provide a tax advantage as well. With an ETF, you only realize a gain or loss when you sell your shares. For long-term investors, this can reduce your taxable capital gains and give you control over when you realize them.

With a mutual fund, transactions in the underlying portfolio generate gains and losses that are passed through to the investors. You may realize a taxable capital gain on your mutual fund holding even if you have never sold any shares. Trading activity varies by fund. In index mutual funds, it is generally low, but all funds must make trades to realign to their index and to meet redemption requests. So mutual funds deliver taxable gains regularly.

The following table illustrates the similarities and differences between ETFs and mutual funds.

	Exchange-Traded Funds (ETFs)	Index Mutual Funds	Actively Managed Mutual Funds
Trading	Throughout the day	End of day	End of day
Valuation	Throughout the day	End of day	End of day
Expenses	Low—often lower than comparable mutual funds	Low	Higher

	Exchange-Traded Funds (ETFs)	Index Mutual Funds	Actively Managed Mutual Funds
Transaction costs	Trading commission the same as stock trades	None if through fund company, varies through other institutions	None if through fund company, varies through other institutions
Management style	Passive	Passive	Active
Diversified within categories	Yes	Yes	Yes
Diversified across categories	No	Available	Available
Minimum investment	One share	Specified dollar amount	Specified dollar amount
Taxable gains	Only on sale	On sale and generated through internal trades	On sale and generated through internal trades

Annuities

Annuities are an investment product issued by insurance companies. To be considered an annuity, the product must offer to pay out a guaranteed monthly income stream either immediately or at some point in the future. There are three broad categories of annuities: **variable annuities, income annuities,** and **deferred annuities.**

Variable annuities allow you to invest in funds that are very similar to mutual funds. These are common options for retirement plans offered in school districts and nonprofit organizations. But you can also invest in them through your financial adviser or insurance agent.

Variable annuities offer additional features beyond what a straight-up mutual fund or ETF can. They often have a guaranteed value that will pay out in the event of your death regardless of the value of the investments you choose, and they offer the opportunity to convert your investments to guaranteed monthly payments. While your money is in the variable annuity contract, all earnings are tax-exempt.

However, variable annuities charge fees to provide the guarantees, and they can be high enough to override the tax advantage of the contract. They also require you to leave your money in the contract for a minimum time, called a surrender period, or risk paying a hefty withdrawal charge. These minimum holding periods can be quite long.

For most, the benefits offered by a variable annuity are outweighed by the costs and complexity. However, a simple low-cost contract may be a good option for those who have maxed out their other available tax-advantaged retirement savings accounts.

While variable annuities are not for everyone, another type of annuity can be a staple part of your portfolio when you are nearing or in retirement. The income annuity provides a guaranteed monthly payment that will feel like you are getting a paycheck. For those who aren't interested in spending time taking care of their investments and worry about making their savings last, the income annuity is a perfect solution.

Income annuities have their drawbacks. You buy an income annuity with a single, sizeable investment. The basic income annuity contract pays you a guaranteed monthly payment for the rest of your life, regardless of how long you live. If you live a good long time, you will get far more back than you put in. If something unforeseen happens and you aren't around very long, there is no return of your investment. The money is locked up, so with a few exceptions, you can't withdraw more than your monthly payment.

There are a variety of contract terms to limit these risks. You can add minimum payment time frames, such as ten or twenty years, to guarantee that a payment will be made for at least that period. Some contracts will pay a benefit to your heirs if you pass away within your guaranteed payment period. To combat the risk that your monthly payment won't keep pace with your bills, there are contracts that will increase your monthly payment each year by a set percentage. However, these features will reduce the size of the monthly payment your investment will buy.

Another relatively simple annuity is the deferred annuity. Deferred annuities pay interest that can be higher than available on other secure investments. In exchange for the higher interest rate, you must lock up your money for a surrender period or pay a penalty. At the end of the surrender period, you can withdraw your money, renew your contract, or convert your investment to guaranteed fixed monthly payments. While invested, your money grows tax-exempt. Deferred annuities can be a good investment as you are preparing for your retirement or as a substitute for bonds.

There are different variations of these contracts, but all annuities fall into one of these basic categories. The information on the following pages summarizes the different annuity contracts.

Variable Annuity

FEATURES

- Mutual fund like investments
- Value fluctuates with underlying investments
- Monthly payment based on balance when payments begin

PROS

- Earnings grow tax-exempt until withdrawn
- May offer a guaranteed death benefit

CONS

- Can be complex
- May have high fees
- Long surrender periods

USES

- Retirement savings if you've maxed out your other options

Income Annuity

FEATURES

- Guaranteed monthly payments for your life or another specified period

PROS

- Monthly income that feels like a paycheck
- Payments guaranteed no matter how long you live unless a shorter time is selected

CONS

- Money is locked up, and with few exceptions, you can't get more than your monthly payment.

- With a basic contract, payments end when you die, regardless of how soon that is. This can be mitigated by adding contract features

USES
- Retirement income

Deferred Annuity
FEATURES
- Guaranteed interest rate for a specific term, usually more than 3 years
- At the end of the term, money can be withdrawn, rolled to a new contract, or converted to an income annuity

PROS
- Offers a guaranteed investment return and flexibility at the end of the contract
- Money grows tax-exempt until withdrawn

CONS
- Money is locked up for the contract term.
- Early withdrawals will incur a surrender charge.

USES
- Conservative investments good for when you are approaching retirement
- A bond substitute

Mutual funds, ETFs, and annuities help you achieve different aspects of your investment goals. Mutual funds and ETFs provide instant diversification within a single asset category or across a wide range of them. Annuities provide guarantees that funds cannot. These investments are not mutually exclusive. They can be combined to achieve whatever your investment goals may be.

Eggs and Baskets: Diversification

Don't put all your eggs in one basket. That adage applies to a lot of life. If we all had crystal balls so we could see the future, we would just do the one best thing. But since we don't, we mix it up. We hedge our bets. We try different things to limit the downside of our decisions.

Diversification is a way of dealing with life's uncertainties, and investment uncertainties are no exception. We don't know what investments will provide the best return, or which ones will turn out to be dogs. So we spread our money around and hope at least some investments will be winners.

Investments that offer diversification are those that perform differently under the same market conditions. While the price of one investment zigs, the other zags. The starkest example of how diversification works can be shown with a simple portfolio of company stock and cash.

Individual company stock prices change minute to minute during business days. The value of cash is always the same. The following table shows how diversification between cash and stock reduces the range of value changes for the combined portfolio relative to a stock-only portfolio.

Portfolio: XYZ Shares		Portfolio: XYZ and Cash	
Initial value	$100	Initial value XYZ	$80
		Initial value Cash	$20

Portfolio: XYZ Shares		Portfolio: XYZ and Cash	
Price change XYZ	+/– 10%	Price change XYZ	+/– 10%
		Price change Cash	+/– 0%
Ending value	$90 or $110	Ending value	$92 or $108

Stocks and cash behave very differently, so cash is the ultimate diversifier. If you invest $100 in a stock and the price goes up by $10, your investment value will be $110. If the stock price goes down by $10, your investment value will be $90. But if you own $80 in stock and $20 in cash, the outcome will be different. For the same percentage fluctuation in value for the stock, you will only gain or lose $8.

The range of outcomes is narrower, with lower gains but also lower losses. Because the range of outcomes is narrower, the risk of the portfolio with cash is lower than the portfolio with stock alone.

Combining different company stocks from different industries will allow negative information about one company or industry to be offset by positive information from other companies, resulting in a portfolio of stocks whose risk is less than that of any single company. However, your portfolio will still be exposed to the risks that impact all companies, like economic growth, interest rates, and regulations.

You can smooth out some of those risks by investing in different investment categories. Just as different company stocks can be combined to diversify a stock portfolio, different types of investments can be combined to provide further diversification, as with the stock and cash example. The values of bonds and hard assets behave differently than stocks and offer more diversification than you would get with stocks from different industries and markets alone.

The various stock markets tend to move together, so you don't get the same diversification there as you do with a completely different investment category. In your company retirement savings plan, you could hold multiple US stock mutual funds and achieve very little diversification. However, you could hold a single mutual fund that invested in stocks and bonds and be fully diversified.

Understanding what the funds invest in is crucial to building a diversified investment strategy. The combination of multiple investment categories into an overall investment strategy is called **asset allocation.**

Pieces of the Pie: Asset Allocation

The biggest influence on portfolio risk is how much is allocated to cash and bonds relative to the allocation to stocks. If you are young and have a long time to invest, a good investment portfolio for you may have 20 percent or less in cash and bonds with the rest in the stock markets. If you are nearer to retirement, your portfolio may have 40 percent or more in cash and bonds.

A generic rule of thumb for determining how much you should have in stocks is to subtract your age from 110. If you are thirty, your portfolio would have 80 percent in stocks and 20 percent in bonds and cash. If you are fifty, your portfolio would have 60 percent in stocks and 40 percent in bonds and cash. This may or may not work for your situation depending on how much you have saved and your other sources of income.

You can develop your own asset allocation based on when you need to spend your money. You want your money to be there when you need to spend it, but at the same time, you want as much of your money working for you as possible. Dividing your spending needs into time frames will help you create an asset allocation that does what it needs to do for you.

Cash has no valuation risk. If you put your cash in a savings account or a money market mutual fund, it will earn interest, and you don't have to worry about it losing any value. But it won't earn much interest, and over time the value of what it can buy will erode with inflation. You wouldn't want to keep much more than what you need to spend in the next year in these accounts. If you are still working, you can reasonably limit your cash holdings to your emergency savings and upcoming larger expenses.

What you will spend in the next one to three years can be invested in short-term bonds or bond mutual funds. Bonds and bond mutual funds will pay higher interest rates than savings accounts or money market mutual funds, but the value of your investment can fluctuate on a daily basis.

Using the yield on a composite of two-year corporate bonds from the Treasury Department as a proxy for short-term bonds, the returns and historical number of periods with losses from 1984 through 2017 are in the following table. Since 1984, there has never been a three-year period that produced a loss in the Treasury Department's two-year bond composite. For holding periods with losses, the losses on a $1,000 investment were less than $30.

Holding Period	Percentage of Periods with Losses
1 month	17.20%
3 months	12.50%

Holding Period	Percentage of Periods with Losses
6 months	7.70%
1 year	1.80%
3 years	0.00%

Source: US Department of the Treasury, "HQM Corporate Bond Yield Curve Par Yields, 1984–Present."

There are 408 one-month periods from 1984 to 2017, so seventy of them would have seen short-term bonds losing money. There are 396 one-year periods, and only in about seven did short-term bonds lose money. There are 372 three-year periods, and in none of them did short-term bonds lose money.

You can be reasonably confident that most if not more than all of your savings for spending in the next one to three years will be there for you. If you are still working, this might be savings for projects or purchases you expect in the next few years. If you are no longer working, this will be what you expect to withdraw from your savings for living expenses.

For money that you will be spending in the next three to ten years, you can pick up some extra interest by investing in intermediate bonds or bond funds. Intermediate bond funds invest in bonds that mature in three to ten years. They usually pay higher interest rates than are paid on short-term bonds. But the longer the time to maturity, the wider the possible fluctuations in prices. Using the Treasury Department's five-year corporate bond composite, the historical percentages of periods with losses are in the following table. For periods longer than three years, there haven't been any losses in value since 1984 either.

Holding Period	Percentage of Periods with Losses
1 month	27.30%
3 months	19.50%
6 months	15.50%
1 year	8.40%
3 years	0.00%

Source: US Department of the Treasury, "HQM Corporate Bond Yield Curve Par Yields, 1984–Present."

If you are still working and planning to continue to do so for more than ten years, you may not need this investment category at all. However, it is an important category if you are no longer working or have just a few years left before retirement.

The most important category for delivering growth in your savings is stocks. But they are also the most likely to deliver losses over short time frames. Since 1950, the average twelve-month return on the S&P 500, including dividends, has been over 12 percent. But the variability of returns has been big. The following table provides the number of periods with losses over different time frames.

Holding Period	Percentage of Periods with Losses
1 month	34.80%
3 months	28.60%

Holding Period	Percentage of Periods with Losses
6 months	25.10%
1 year	21.60%
3 years	11.30%
5 years	9.00%
10 years	3.70%

Source: Shiller and Kase, "U.S. Stock Markets 1871–Present and CAPE Ratio"

Even after ten years, there is still a chance that you will have less money than you started with in stocks, but historically that hasn't happened very often. Three-quarters of ten-year periods since 1950 have provided a return greater than 7 percent per year. There were 696 ten-year periods from 1950 and 2017, so more than 522 of them would have provided a return greater than 7 percent. You can reasonably invest the money that you won't be spending for at least ten years in the equity markets, and that will provide growth in your investments to help your money last.

People in the early years of their career won't need to spend their retirement savings for decades, so most of it can be invested in stock markets. Those near retirement will still need their money to last for twenty or thirty years, so even they can afford to invest half or more of their savings in stocks.

The following table summarizes how to allocate your money based on when you will spend it.

Category	Time Before You Spend
Money market/savings	Less than 1 year
Short-term bonds or bond funds	1–3 years
Intermediate term bonds or bond funds	3–10 years
Stocks or stock funds	10 years or more

Bad Timing

What would be really great is if we could invest more money in the stock markets when they are going up and get out of the stock markets when they are going down. Our return would be much better if we could avoid those nasty market downturns. Many attempt to do just that, but few are any good at it.

The trouble is if you missed just the months with the top 5 percent of returns in the market since 1950, you would have cut your returns almost in half. Of course, if you were able to avoid the bottom 5 percent of months in the process, you would perform just about as well as the market. But given the uncertainty of when those occur, that doesn't seem like a good trade-off.

In an analysis by Dalbar done in 2011, the twenty-year annualized investment return for the average investor was just 2.1 percent when the S&P 500 was up 7.8 percent and a prominent bond index, the Barclays Aggregate Bond Index, was up 6.5 percent.[157] How does that happen?

Cameron knows how this goes. He makes good money as the chief financial officer of a family-owned company. He's been able to save a lot of money over the years, but his balances aren't what they should be. His main goal in investing his savings for many years was to simply make a lot of money so he and his wife, Taylor, could retire early. They won't be able to retire as early as he hoped.

His biggest mistake was trying to time the market. He frequently bailed on his stock positions when the market was declining only to stay out of the market too long and miss the subsequent upswing.

For the three years following the financial crisis, he was mostly out of the stock market. As a result, he missed what could have been a cumulative 95 percent increase had he been invested in an S&P 500 index mutual fund.

Cameron was not alone. The peak in value for the S&P 500 prior to the crisis came in September of 2007. From there the stock market began a gradual decline, with some investors selling sporadically. However, in September of 2008, the floodgates opened, and mutual fund investors began pouring out of equity funds. The S&P 500 had already lost more than 36 percent of its value.

The bottom of the market came in February of 2009, just four months and 16 percent later. But money kept leaving the stock markets. Even as the stock market crested its prior peak, equity funds saw growing withdrawals through the end of 2012. The chart on the next page shows cumulative net money flowing into (positive) or out of (negative) equity mutual funds and the S&P 500 Total Return Index throughout the market decline and recovery.

If you had perfect foresight, you would have sold in September of 2007 at the peak. You would have avoided the following drop in value of 51 percent. Then you would have bought back your investment at the low in February of 2009. If you had done that, then ten years later—by September 2017—your investment would have risen by almost four times, or 14.2 percent per year.

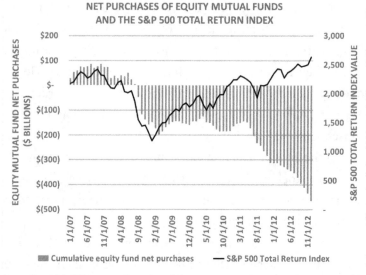

NET PURCHASES OF EQUITY MUTUAL FUNDS
AND THE S&P 500 TOTAL RETURN INDEX

Source: DataHub, "US Investor Flow of Funds into Investment Classes (Bonds, Equities etc.)"; Yahoo Finance, "S&P 500 Total Return Index."

But be realistic. You only have perfect hindsight. You know nothing about the future. You can't tell whether the market is at a peak or just a nice viewpoint along the way. And you certainly can't tell when the market has hit bottom.

The biggest monthly net sale of equity funds was in October of 2008, and the biggest monthly net buy following that was January of 2013. If you had sold and bought back in those months, as many other market participants did, your return for the ten years ending in September 2017 would have been just 10 percent, or about 1 percent per year.

What if you had done nothing? If you had not touched your stock market investments, in the following ten years your money would have more than doubled for an annualized return of 7.3 percent. Doing nothing is certainly easier than picking both the top and bottom of the stock market. Steadily adding to your investments, as you would in your retirement account, would have been even better.

Timing the market is a fool's game. Seeing your nest egg shrink is no fun for anyone, but if you don't have to spend your money right away, it can recover. Putting only money you won't need to spend for a good long time in risky, growth-oriented, stock market investments allows you to weather the market's worst.

Staying Balanced

The markets don't stay in one place, and once you've decided on how you want to invest your money, you have to pay attention to it. Left unattended, your overall investment portfolio will likely become riskier, since the portion of your money invested in stocks will grow faster than that invested in bonds and cash over time. While your balance grows, the portion of your balance occupied by stocks will get bigger.

To keep your risk where you want it, you have to occasionally **rebalance**. If stocks have become a bigger portion of your portfolio than you intended, you can sell enough to take the balance down to where you want it. You would invest the proceeds in the categories in your portfolio that were smaller than you wanted them to be.

The average investor tends to buy into the stock market when it is near its peak and sell when it is near its low.[158] Rebalancing can help you avoid that. It causes you to sell investments that have gone up and buy investments that have either declined in value or not gone up by as much. The old "buy low, sell high" rule is put into action when your natural tendency is to buy high and sell low. Rebalancing regularly has been shown to add returns above the returns of portfolios that were not rebalanced.[159]

No One Right Answer

Investing in the financial markets according to when you will use your money is one way to invest your savings. Time-based investing is a rule of thumb that generally works, but there are lots of other strategies that can work too. If you have an expertise in managing some other kind of investment, there is no reason you shouldn't pursue that.

Ravi plowed all his savings into apartment buildings while he continued to work at his corporate job. He struggled with his first two investments, but as he figured the business out, it became more profitable. He began using the profits from the first two buildings to buy others and eventually had enough income that he could quit his job to run his business.

His investments are not diversified. They are concentrated in real estate in the Portland metro area. But it is a business in which Ravi has become an expert, so he feels confident that the cash flow and gains on the real estate will support him now and throughout his life.

Not all small business ventures make good investments for retirement savings. Ravi's business is uniquely suited as a source of both current and future income. The properties have intrinsic value that will grow over time, and they provide a steady flow of cash. As his business grows, Ravi can leave more of the day-to-day management to employees, giving him a great deal of flexibility.

A business that depends on you being active for it to generate an income is not a good investment for retirement savings. If you have this type of business, you need to be saving and investing separately to assure that you can pay your bills when you are no longer able to be active in it.

There are lots of ways to invest your savings. The crucial part is having savings to begin with. Ravi couldn't have bought his first apartment buildings without building up enough savings to make the investment. If you have expertise and a passion for

Josie

Josie has had a few advisers tell her that her investment strategy is all wrong for her. It is unconventional, especially for someone on the verge of retirement, but it works. Josie has her retirement savings entirely invested in dividend-paying stocks that she has selected herself. That flies in the face of the typical investment advice to take a more conservative investment approach as you near the time when you need to spend your money. But conventional wisdom isn't the only wisdom. Josie understands her risks and how to manage them.

The reason that her strategy works is because the portfolio throws off enough in dividends to support Josie's lifestyle when combined with Social Security. In fact, due to how much savings she has accumulated over her career, between the two she'll have more income than she needs. That means she doesn't have to sell her stocks to cover her living expenses.

Since she doesn't face the risk of selling in a down market to cover day-to-day expenses, the investment strategy will work for her. Things could still go wrong. The companies she owns could lower their dividends. She could have an expense that outstrips her emergency savings and causes her to sell some of her holdings at a bad time. But her diversified portfolio limits the impact of any actions a single company takes, and her emergency savings provide at least a partial buffer to selling stocks into a down market.

The other downside of Josie's strategy is she must pay attention to her investments. She monitors thirty companies closely and keeps tabs on another ten as possible future investments. It takes a good chunk of her free time, but she enjoys the research.

She is willing to keep up the work for the time being, and she'll have even more time to do it once she leaves her job. She's been investing this way for a long time and knows what is involved. She does anticipate needing to move to a simpler mutual fund strategy in the future, when she tires of doing the work herself. But for now, what she's doing is working.

managing your savings in a way that isn't ordinarily advised, there is nothing wrong with that. But make sure you really know what you are getting into and have a backup plan if things don't pan out as you expect.

There is a vast array of investment opportunities available. They can be complex and difficult to sift through. Investing on your own takes a lot of time and information. It requires a level of expertise that many simply do not have. There is no shame in realizing that you are not an investment expert. If you do not have the time, the expertise, or the resources to invest on your own, hire a professional.

Vocabulary

Stocks: Shares of stock reflect partial ownership in a company. Long-term values are driven by growth in earnings and dividends, but short-term, just about any news can have an impact.

Bonds: Loans to companies or governments. Values are driven by changes in interest rates, the time remaining to maturity, and the credit worthiness of the issuer.

Hard assets: Things you can touch, like real estate, gold, and agricultural and energy products.

Pooled investments: Investment products where money from many investors is combined to buy a portfolio of investments. Mutual funds and exchange-traded funds (ETFs) are among several pooled investment products.

Actively managed funds: Funds where the investment manager is trying to produce an investment return that is better than a benchmark index.

Index: A fixed list of investments. The S&P 500 is an index that contains the 500 largest US companies. There are hundreds of indices representing all corners of the investment universe.

Index funds: Passively managed funds where the investment manager is trying to mimic the return of an index.

Variable annuities: Contracts that allow you to invest in mutual fund–like investments while offering a variety of guarantees for which you pay.

Income annuities: Contracts that pay a guaranteed monthly payment for the rest of your life or a set period.

Deferred annuities: Contracts that pay a guaranteed interest rate for a specified time. The contract can be converted to an income annuity or rolled to a new contract, or you can withdraw your money at the end of the period.

Asset allocation: The combination of different investment categories into an overall investment strategy.

Rebalancing: Maintaining your asset allocation by selling investments that have grown beyond your target allocation and buying investments that have fallen below your target allocation.

Main Ideas

1. Aside from cash and other safe ways to hold your money, there are three primary investment categories: stocks, bonds, and hard assets. Stocks and bonds are the foundation of a sound investment strategy. Hard assets are not required and, if used, should be used sparingly.
2. You can invest in anything through pooled investment products, like mutual funds and exchange-traded funds.
3. You get the most diversification by combining investments that behave differently from one another at any given time.
4. Most of your investment risk is determined by how much you have invested in stocks versus bonds and cash.
5. There is no single best way to invest your money; however, a strategy based on when you will need to spend your money generally works.

Chapter 11

You Don't Have to Master Investing

WHEN I WAS YOUNG AND SINGLE, I USED TO DRIVE FROM MY San Francisco Bay Area home to Lake Tahoe to ski on winter weekends. On many occasions the mountain passes required chains or traction tires due to icy conditions. Guessing that my sporty convertible Mercury Capri did not have traction tires, a concerned friend once asked me if I knew how to put on tire chains. I said, "Sure, all you do is hang a twenty-dollar bill out the window."

On snowy weekends a gang of opportunistic people converged on the designated chain-up areas along the highway to help motorists put on their chains. For twenty bucks these folks would have your chains on your car in ten minutes flat. There was no need to get wet, cold, and dirty and no real need to know exactly how it was done.

These days, investing your savings in a perfectly reasonable way can be like hanging a twenty-dollar bill out the window. There are many low-cost products and services that will do exactly what you need them to do without you having to know much about investing. That leaves you to concentrate on saving enough.

Timing Is Everything: Target-Date Mutual Funds

In 1994, Wells Fargo and Barclays Global Investors created what has become a staple in employer-sponsored retirement savings plans, the **target-date retirement fund**.[160] The product was created in response to concerns that participants in 401(k) and other similar savings plans weren't investing their savings well.

Regardless of the education seminars offered or the quality of the materials, participants made terrible mistakes in their investments that jeopardized their financial security. They tended to diversify poorly, creating portfolios that were either too risky or not risky enough. They bought high and sold low, so investment returns for participants tended to be paltry. On average, they were much lower than returns found in professionally managed pension plans.[161]

Target-date retirement funds are fully diversified, holding a mix of US and foreign stocks, bonds, and in some cases, hard assets. These funds were designed to take the investment decision-making out of participants' hands and put it into the hands of professional managers.

The funds generally come in a series with retirement dates every five years from the nearest current retirement fund out to a date far enough in the future to accommodate even the youngest eligible workers. You will recognize the target-date funds in your retirement plan because the series will have a year in the name of the fund. The names might be something like Target Retirement 2030. The 2030 represents the approximate year of expected retirement.

In developing any investment strategy, the most important piece of information is how long you have. The longer you have before you need to spend your money, the greater risk you can take with your investments. Greater risk generally means higher returns over time. Regardless of how much other information you consider, time will always play the most important role in determining what is the best mix of investments for you.

Target-date retirement funds use this fact to your advantage. These funds are designed to be one-stop investment alternatives you can hold for your entire career. As the retirement year approaches, the proportion of the fund invested in stocks declines and the proportion invested in bonds and cash increases. This makes the fund less risky—though definitely not risk-free—over time. You simply choose the fund with a target date that is closest to your likely retirement date.

To be clear, the funds remain invested even after the target date. No one will send you a check in the year of the fund. However, your savings will be invested in a reasonable way for someone who is living on their savings.

More than 70 percent of retirement savings plans offer target-date retirement funds.[162] In many plans, the funds are the default investment option. Default options are the investments where your employer deposits your contributions if you don't make any selections yourself.

While target-date funds made their debut in 401(k) plans, you can buy them in any type of account, including IRAs and taxable accounts. They are widely available at most financial institutions. Similar funds are also available in many state-sponsored 529 college savings plans. These age-based funds move to low-risk investments as your child approaches college age.

Comparing Target-Date Funds

Not all target-date funds are created equal. There are three primary areas where target-date funds differ: the investment strategy the fund uses, whether the allocation is actively or passively managed, and what the investment expenses are.

The investment strategy and how it changes over time is called the **glide path**. Different managers use different glide paths. Funds with dates far in the future will generally hold at least 80 percent in risky stock market investments. But funds can differ in how much risk they take as the retirement date gets closer. The average allocation to stock markets at the retirement date across the industry is about 50 percent, but it ranges between 30 and 70 percent.[163]

For most, a 50 percent allocation to stocks when you retire is reasonable. It provides enough opportunity for growth to sustain a retiree's spending through a long retirement while allowing enough stability to make current withdrawals manageable. A lower allocation to stocks could result in returns too low for your savings to last.

The second big difference among funds is whether the underlying investments are actively or passively managed. Actively managed funds try to perform better than market indices by choosing what the managers hope to be better-performing investments. Passively managed funds invest to mimic the market indices in the various investment categories used by the funds.

With an actively managed fund, your investments may perform better than the average of the underlying investments' benchmark market indices, or they may perform worse. With a passively managed fund, you will basically get the average of the market indices' performance less the fund's expenses.

Fund expenses are the third area where target date funds vary. Actively managed funds generally have higher expenses than passively managed funds. Since their invention, most target-date money has flowed into actively managed funds. But lower fees are driving growth in passive funds, making them more common.

Cash flows into passive funds have grown at a 25 percent annual pace, and they currently represent 32 percent of total assets invested in target-date funds.[164]

In your work-related retirement savings plan, you won't have any choice of which fund company's series to choose. Your employer will have done that for you. The good news is that three fund companies, Fidelity, T. Rowe Price, and Vanguard, have nearly three-quarters of the money invested in target retirement funds, and all of them have reasonable glide paths and fees.[165]

There is a good chance your employer's plan uses one of these series. If not, look closely at the glide path and the fees, which will be provided in a fund fact sheet. A fact sheet is a single-page summary of the fund's investment strategy, fees, and history. You will find it either online or in the plan materials provided to you.

As already mentioned, the investment strategy at the point of retirement should have around 50 percent in stocks. A lower allocation may not allow your money to grow as it needs to, and a significantly higher allocation could make taking withdrawals from the fund early in retirement risky.

You can find out how the fund's fees compare to similar funds in the industry by searching on the internet for the fund name and selecting the search result from Morningstar. They compare the fund's fees to funds in the same category. If fees seem high, choosing a different investment option may be worthwhile. The average total fees for target retirement funds ranged from 0.67 percent to 0.77 percent in 2017, depending on how far out the retirement date was.[166] Dates further in the future have higher expenses.

The following table summarizes what to look for in a target-date retirement fund.

	Fund Characteristic	What to Look For
Glide path	Allocation to stocks ranges from 30% to 70% at retirement date.	Look for fund series with 50% in stocks at retirement date.
Active vs. passive	Active funds try to outperform the blended markets in which they invest. Passive funds try to mimic the blended markets in which they invest.	Active funds are more expensive and may outperform or underperform. Passive funds are less expensive, and you'll get what the market delivers.
Fees	Average total expenses are 0.67% to 0.77% depending on the time to the retirement date.	If fees are significantly higher, keep looking.

Beyond your company-sponsored retirement plan, you do have choices. If you are saving in an individual retirement account or other account that isn't tax-advantaged, you can still invest in a target-date retirement fund.

What the Critics Say

Target-date funds have their detractors. They were particularly sharply criticized following the financial crisis and labeled as too risky. Funds for near retirees—in other words, the funds with the nearest retirement dates—lost value during the crisis. There were a few that were down over 30 percent at points during the six months the crisis was in full swing.

Even the most conservative funds held substantial allocations to stocks. Stock market indices were down more than 25 percent just in September and October of 2008, the first two months of the crisis. To make matters worse, the lower-risk corporate bond holdings in these funds were also down more than 7 percent in those two months. Stock markets continued to decline through February of 2009, though corporate bonds recovered somewhat.

Target-date funds are not guaranteed. They don't provide a monthly payout when you retire. They simply provide an appropriate investment strategy for your age. If you were investing in the investment categories separately, a prudent investment strategy would still put 50 to 60 percent of your savings in risky stock markets when you are near retirement. A 50 percent stock and 50 percent bond allocation was what William Bengen used in testing his 4 percent rule, which was described in chapter 4.[167]

Even for near retirees, the typical investment strategy for the target retirement fund is appropriate for the long time you need your money to last. The intention of your retirement savings is to accumulate enough money to last you for at least twenty-five to thirty years, and that time horizon needs a big dose of stocks to provide the growth that will help the money last.

The downside is, given the typical proportion in stock markets, these funds will lose value in about two out of every ten years. If your first year in retirement is one of these two and your first withdrawal is a large portion of your account, your savings may not recover.

The problem, however, isn't with the investment strategy. The problem is that not enough has been saved. In order to withstand the risk of any stock market investment, whether as part of a target date fund or separately, you have to have enough set aside so withdrawals in any given year are relatively small. In your early years, withdrawals of 4 percent of the balance should be your goal.

Target date funds offer a single managed alternative that will give you an investment that will be reasonably appropriate for you given when you expect to retire. You don't need to do anything with it because the fund manager maintains the investment strategy. As you approach your retirement date, the fund will become more conservative. If you are near retirement and you will be drawing down your balance quickly, target-date funds are not the right choice for you. But for many, they are a sensible way to invest your retirement savings.

Humans Need Not Apply: Automated Investment Solutions

An alternative to a single target-date retirement fund is a **managed account**. In a managed account, an adviser will select investments for you from available options, allocating your savings based on answers you provide about your savings balances, tolerance for market ups and downs, and most importantly how long you have before you withdraw the money. You can get this service on the cheap if you don't mind that your adviser isn't human.

Automated investment services have been around for more than twenty years. Financial Engines pioneered automated advice to 401(k) participants beginning in 1996.[168] The services are a growing option in workplace retirement savings plans, with 55 percent of plans surveyed by Aon Hewitt offering one in 2015.[169]

Automated investment services became more widely available outside retirement plans beginning in 2008. These services are somewhat derogatorily called **robo-advisers**.

The task of creating a well-diversified investment portfolio is largely a math problem. The key is to combine investment categories that behave differently from one another in different market environments. Using the historical returns or expectations for future market returns and a statistical measure of how the categories' returns relate to one another, a good combination for a given time horizon can be calculated. Since a reasonable investment allocation can be made mathematically, this part of the investment process is well suited to an automated solution.

Managed account services in employer-sponsored retirement savings plans, like 401(k)s, will invest your savings in some of the funds available to you in your plan using an automated system to determine the proportions to allocate to each fund. They will gradually reduce your investment in risky stock markets as you get closer to your retirement date, like a target-date fund. There are fees associated with the service. You may have to pay them from your balance, or in some cases, your employer may pay them on your behalf.

Outside your work-related retirement savings plan, either for your IRA accounts or other savings, robo-advisers offer inexpensive investment management. These advisers generally use exchange-traded index funds or index mutual funds, so the investment expenses are low. Because the investments are maintained automatically, there is no human to pay, and therefore the fees charged by the advisers are low too (some are even free). That leaves more of your investment return for you.

The table on the next page compares two of the top-rated robo-advisers.

There are many other robo-advisers, and as time passes more will surely come on the scene. Both managed account services and robo-advisers are held to the same regulatory standards as human registered investment advisers. However, these automated services are willing to work with very small balances, and their fees are a fraction of the average fees charged by advisers. They are a good solution for any saver.

	Betterment[a]	Wealthfront[b]
Number of investment categories	12	11
Fees for service	Range between 0.15% for accounts with more than $100,000 and 0.35% for accounts with less than $10,000	0.25%
Investment expenses	0.13%	0.12%
All-in annual cost on $10,000 account	$48	$37

a. Betterment home page, accessed January 31, 2017, https://www.betterment.com/.
b. Wealthfront home page, accessed January 31, 2017, https://www.wealthfront.com/.

A Piece of Advice: Working with a Financial Adviser

While fees do take a bite out of your savings, sometimes it's just worthwhile to pay for some advice. Fixing a short in your home electrical wiring yourself is cheap, but the results could prove to be disastrous unless you're an electrician. Similarly, you might need some help creating and managing your own financial plan unless you are trained to do it.

The trick is getting the right kind of advice and having the right expectations. As you've seen, the investment piece of the equation can be automated. You can get good investment management for a low price through a target retirement fund or a robo-adviser. Where you can use help that will be worth paying more for is in creating a financial plan.

Here is a list of what the plan should include:

- A comprehensive picture of your current finances, including current savings, debt, and income
- Your financial goals, including retirement, funding college for your kids, and any other goals you may have
- A budget and savings plan to help you reach your financial goals
- An analysis and recommendations for your insurance needs, including property insurance, life and disability insurance, and possibly long-term care insurance
- If retirement is nearer, a plan for your withdrawals from savings and options for making your savings last
- A strategy to minimize your tax burden while meeting your financial goals
- An investment strategy that will best help you meet your goals with a plan for how the strategy will change over time
- Guidance for preparing a plan for what happens to your savings when you pass away, called an estate plan

Some financial planners will do just a plan for a fixed fee or hourly rate. The fixed fees for a financial plan can range from $1,500 to $5,000 depending on the complexity. Planners typically spend up to fifteen hours on an initial plan, and with average hourly rates of $200, that pans out to about $3,000.[170] Others will include financial planning as a service when they manage your investments for a fee based on your assets under management. Asset-based fees range depending on the size of your portfolio, but the following table provides the national averages. These fees don't include expenses associated with the specific investments, such as mutual fund expense ratios or transaction costs.

Assets under Management ($)	Annual Fee (%)	Annual Fee ($)
100,000	1.12	1,120
250,000	1.07	2,675
500,000	1.05	5,250
1,000,000	1.02	10,200
2,000,000	0.94	18,200
5,000,000	0.84	42,000

Source: Advisory HQ, "Average Financial Advisor Fees & Costs: 2017-2018 Report."

Even with asset-based fees, if your adviser is providing the planning listed, they are well worth the money. It takes at least $250,000 in assets under management to cover the financial planning costs, so it's no wonder that advisers are reluctant to take accounts this size or smaller.

Plenty of advisers will charge these fees and more to provide nothing but investment management. So often people don't realize the need for a plan and that they should be getting much more for their money.

To find an adviser who will provide a plan, look for someone with the **Certified Financial Planner (CFP)** designation. People with this designation have been through a comprehensive course of study covering all areas that are important to your financial security. They must have experience. They have to practice for three years before they can use the CFP designation. They also must submit a plan to the Certified

Kara

Kara was planning to leave her adviser when she asked for a second opinion on her investments. She had two concerns. First, she said she didn't think her investments were performing well. They certainly weren't beating the market, and the investments she managed herself in her 401(k) had performed better. Second, she didn't feel like she had a good understanding of whether she and her husband were on track to meet their financial goals. She was most focused on the first concern, but it was the second that was more important.

Her adviser was managing her investments, but he wasn't helping her achieve her goals. To do that, Kara's adviser should have provided a plan for growing her savings enough so that she and her husband could retire when they wanted. Since savings grow from both contributions and market returns, the adviser should have been comparing actual contributions to planned contributions. When talking about the investments, he should have been comparing the investment returns to planned returns as well as market returns. He should have provided regular snapshots of where Kara and her husband were relative to the milestones in the plan as well as solutions and expectations for managing any shortfalls. His advice should have been far more comprehensive, covering her insurance and estate planning needs.

Without this broader perspective, Kara was uncertain about her progress and was left to draw conclusions about her investment results from information that wasn't relevant. Assuming that her adviser's investment should beat "the market" didn't address whether the returns she was getting were meeting her needs.

Kara's comparison of her return on her 401(k) savings also led to the wrong conclusion. Her biggest investment in her 401(k) was her company's stock. The fact that her company's stock had done better than her adviser-recommended, broadly diversified portfolio was pure luck.

Had Kara's adviser provided a more comprehensive service, complete with a financial plan, she would have been more likely to feel like she was getting her money's worth. She also would have had more confidence that she and her husband could reach their goals, and she would have better understood how the investments fit into that picture. While it turned out that the adviser's investment strategy was reasonable for Kara's situation, he still lost the account because he hadn't given Kara what she needed.

Financial Planners Board of Standards to demonstrate their knowledge and skill.

About a third of CFPs do planning for all clients they work with.[171] Financial planners in your area can be found through www.letsmakeaplan.org, a Certified Financial Planners Board of Standards site. Another good source is the National Association of Personal Financial Advisors, or NAPFA (www.napfa.org). This is an association of fee-only financial advisers. **Fee-only advisers** only receive the fees you pay them. They don't receive commissions or other payments associated with any particular recommendations they make.

There is no need to master the world of investments yourself. Like any other specialty, getting the help of a professional is usually worthwhile. Reasonable help for managing your investments can be found at a low cost through a target-date retirement fund or a robo-adviser. You can get a professionally managed portfolio for any size account at a very affordable rate. When you are ready for advice, make sure it's the right kind. Where you can really use the advice is in creating a financial plan that will help you reach your goals and protect what you achieve.

Vocabulary

Target-date retirement funds: Fully diversified mutual funds whose underlying investments gradually become more conservative as the fund approaches its target date, which is expected to be the approximate year the investor plans to retire.

Glide path: A projection of how the investment allocation for a target-date retirement fund changes as the target date approaches.

Managed account: An adviser will select investments for you based on the available options and the answers you provide regarding how long you plan to leave the money invested and how much investment risk you can tolerate.

Robo-advisers: Automated managed account services.

Certified Financial Planner (CFP): A designation given to advisers who have undergone a rigorous course of study, have completed at least three years of practice, and have had their work judged to be competent by the Certified Financial Planners Board of Standards.

Fee-only advisers: Advisers who are paid solely from the fee they charge you. They receive no compensation from the providers of the investments they recommend.

Main Ideas

1. Target-date retirement funds are mutual funds whose investment strategy changes over time to become more conservatively managed as the target date approaches. They offer a reasonable investment strategy for the time horizon targeted. All you have to do is contribute to the fund.

2. A target-date fund should still have around 50 percent invested in the stock market at the point of retirement in order to provide the growth you need to make your money last.

3. Managed account services, which may be available through your retirement plan at work, direct your investments automatically based on your time horizon and ability to deal with the market's ups and downs. The service will use the investment options available in the plan.

4. Robo-advisers are an automated investment solution available outside work-related retirement plans that you can use for your IRA or taxable investment accounts. They use low-cost index ETFs or mutual funds and charge very low fees for their advice.

5. When seeking advice from an adviser, look for someone who will provide you with a comprehensive financial plan, not just investment management. Certified Financial Planners (CFPs) have in-depth training in creating financial plans and must demonstrate their skills to a board of standards.

Chapter 12

The Afterlife

JUST AS SETTING YOURSELF UP FOR A LONG LIFE IN RETIREMENT is crucial, so is planning for the chance you won't make it that far. Making the hard decisions now about what will happen with your money, your belongings, your children, and you while you can is the ultimate act of love and responsibility.

There are important documents that allow you to record your wishes and intentions well in advance. In addition, there are products that will help keep your family financially secure. No financial plan is complete before it is rounded out with a will, the right insurance, and authorizations for those who love you to help when needed. These documents together are called your **estate plan.**

Where There's a Will, There's a Way

A will is a document that records what should be done with your savings and other belongings, also known as your assets, if you die. It can take any form, but to be valid it must be witnessed by two disinterested people. A disinterested person is anyone who won't benefit from the will.

A Gallup poll showed that more than half of adults do not have a will or estate plan. More surprising is that nearly half of Americans age fifty-five to sixty-four, and two-thirds of those age forty-five to fifty-four, don't have one.[172] Even if you don't have much, you still want to control what happens to it. Everyone needs a will.

If you haven't left instructions for how to deal with your assets, the state where you live will make the decisions for you. Each state has a set of rules for how to distribute them. Regardless of what you might want or have told your family and friends, the state will follow their rules.

In some states, the rules may be far from what you would want. For example, in many states, your surviving spouse might have to split your assets with your parents and siblings if you haven't left a will indicating otherwise. If you have children and both you and your spouse have died, the state will appoint a guardian according to their rules, and that might not be who you intended. In most states, your children will automatically inherit a portion of your assets, but if they are under the age of eighteen, the court will administer (for a fee) their share. That can make it unnecessarily difficult for your spouse or your children's guardian to access the money needed to raise them.

A will can go a long way toward making life easier for those you've left behind. To have an attorney prepare one is going to cost around $1,000, but it could be more depending on where you live. There are online resources for preparing a will that are less expensive. Rocket Lawyer and LegalZoom are two well-known sites. A will you create yourself online can run less than $100 and may be all you need if you don't have much in the way of assets and have no children. You would be well served to have an attorney review it though. Small mistakes can have big consequences, and a simple review will be less costly than the full preparation.

If you don't have a will yet, make getting one a priority. The time it will take you to prepare one will be far less than the time your family will have to spend sorting things out if you don't.

Your Money or Your Life Insurance

More than 80 percent of people believe you should have life insurance.[173] It is something that you need for some phases of your life but not all. The purpose of life insurance is to replace your income if you are no longer around. You only need life insurance if you have an income and someone else is depending on it to maintain their lifestyle.

Early in your career, you have a lot of earning years ahead of you and a need to save for the future. If you have a spouse or children who depend on your income, life insurance can replace it and provide the savings you would have provided if you die unexpectedly. As your savings grow and you approach retirement, you need less life insurance. When you retire, you no longer have an income to replace, so you no longer need life insurance at all.

If any of the following situations describe you, you need life insurance.

1. **You have young children.** If you have young children, you likely need a lot of life insurance. You will want your children to grow up with the comfortable lifestyle that you hope to provide for them, and you don't want to make life financially difficult for your partner or their guardians.

   You are also most likely to be underinsured. The life insurance provided by your employer will definitely not be enough. Most of those policies only cover one to two years of your salary, and that won't be enough to raise your kids. The younger your children are, the more financial support they will need.

If you or your partner is not working for pay outside the home while you raise the children, you still need life insurance on that person. If the one who isn't working passes away unexpectedly while the children are young, there will be extra expenses for childcare and other things the stay-at-home parent does, and life insurance can provide the money to pay for it.

2. **You are married, and your lifestyle is dependent on your income.** If your partner could not maintain his or her lifestyle without your income, even if you don't have children, you need life insurance. You may need to supplement your partner's income and provide the retirement savings that you would have saved if you had continued to work. If you have debts, those will need to be paid off.

3. **You have outstanding private student loans.**If you have outstanding private student loans, someone may be liable for their payment after you die. If a parent, grandparent, or someone else cosigned for your loan, they may still have to pay the debt after your death. If you live in a community property state and took on the loans after you married, your spouse may still have to pay.

   Federal student loans and parents' PLUS loans, which are available for graduate students or the parents of undergraduate students, are fully discharged upon the death of the borrower or, in the case of the PLUS loan, the student.[174]

This is certainly not an exhaustive list, but it boils down to whether someone will miss your income. If so, you need life insurance. Once you've determined that you need life insurance, the next step is to figure out how much. Lifehappens.org has a good calculator that considers all the relevant information to help you determine how much life insurance you need to put in place.

If any of the following situations describe you, then you do not need life insurance.

1. **You are single, and no one is depending on your income.** While many will miss you, no one will miss your income. Therefore you don't need life insurance.
2. **You are near or in retirement and have the savings you need.** You won't be earning an income anymore, so you won't have an income to replace. Therefore you don't need life insurance.
3. **You are a child.** Children don't need life insurance. They don't have an income to replace. Some insurance companies sell policies pitched as a way to save for college. The cash value can be borrowed when your child is ready for college, and the policy won't be counted as assets for financial aid purposes. But your child doesn't need life insurance, and the expenses to provide it cut into your college savings.

    Saving through a college 529 plan or directly with a mutual fund company will likely leave you with more for your kids' education. An account in your name with the child as beneficiary or in the name of the child will be counted as parental assets on the Free Application for Federal Student Aid (FAFSA), but the first $20,000 is exempt from the Expected Family Contribution (EFC). The EFC is capped at 5.64 percent of parental assets.[175]

Types of Life Insurance

Life insurance comes in two major forms, **term life** and **whole life** insurance. Whole life insurance is also sometimes called permanent life insurance.

With term life insurance, you pay to be insured for a specific term, like ten or twenty years. Your premium will remain the same for that period. When the period is up, if you still need life insurance, you can renew your policy. Your premium for the same insurance will likely increase at that time, mainly because you are older, but if your savings have grown, you will need less insurance. You can cancel your policy at any time without penalty, and if you stop making premium payments, your policy will be automatically canceled.

Whole life insurance has no time limit. The insurance policy will pay out on your death regardless of how old you are if you have kept up the premium payments. The premiums remain level throughout your life. This is a benefit to those who continue to need life insurance when they are older. To make a level premium possible, the premiums are higher than term life premiums, especially while you are young. The extra premiums early on build up an account that the insurance company can invest and use to cover their risk later in your life.

This account will be available as a cash value to you once it gets large enough. You can withdraw the cash value, or you can borrow against it. Any amount you withdraw or borrow reduces your death benefit. The following table compares the features of term and whole life insurance.

	Term Life	Whole Life
Choice of policy length	Yes—10 to 20 years common	No
Provides lifelong coverage	No—only for the term	Yes
Premium remains the same	Yes—for the term	Yes

	Term Life	Whole Life
Low premium	Yes	No
Life insurance benefit guaranteed	Yes	Yes
Accumulates cash value	No	Yes
May be eligible for dividends	No	Yes

Whole, or permanent, life insurance isn't usually necessary. While it's harder to qualify for term life insurance as you get older, if you are saving as you should, you simply won't need the insurance after you retire.

Permanent life insurance is important if you will continue to need to supplement your savings for a spouse or other dependent after you retire. As an example, you may continue to need life insurance if the loss of your Social Security benefit upon your death would cause a hardship for your spouse. Because whole life is permanent, you won't risk being disqualified for it as you get older, and the premiums will stay level.

Whole life insurance also comes in handy if your savings are so large that your heirs will incur estate taxes upon your and your spouse's death. Any of your savings that your spouse inherits are tax-free. However, if your savings inherited by others will be more than the federal and state exemptions, your heirs will pay estate taxes. The federal exemption was $5.49 million in 2017. Many states have much lower exemptions. To avoid paying estate taxes, you can put savings you want to transfer to others above the tax exemption into a whole life insurance policy. The policy will earn interest, and life insurance benefits don't incur taxes.

Early in your career, when your kids are young and you are building your savings, you need life insurance. But as your kids and your savings grow, your need for life insurance will gradually decline until it no longer exists. If you are nearing the end of your career and you have the savings you and your spouse will need to live on, you don't need life insurance.

To the Beneficiaries Go the Spoils

Your life insurance, as well as your retirement accounts, are special. Their distribution is not determined by your will. Upon your death, your life insurance (both private and work-related), your 401(k) or other employer-sponsored retirement account, your IRA, and any other insurance product benefits will be distributed to your beneficiary. It does not matter what your will says.

This sounds great. One less thing to worry about. However, if you don't keep your beneficiaries up to date, it can be a disaster. Make sure your beneficiary designations are correct. Whenever you have a life change, revisit the beneficiaries of your work-related life insurance, your work-related retirement savings, your IRAs, and any other life insurance or annuity policies you own. Do not make your minor children beneficiaries. Children under the age of eighteen cannot receive retirement account distributions or insurance proceeds. These accounts will be held by the financial institution providing them until the children come of age.

Withdrawals from the account are possible for the children's welfare, but the process can require a court order. That makes it time consuming and difficult for your children's guardian to

Carol

Carol and Dave had only been married a couple of years. They were looking forward to many years together in retirement. It was a second marriage for them both, and they felt they were embarking on a whole new life.

They were all set to retire. Carol had some savings, as did Dave. Most of Dave's savings were in a 401(k). They owned their beautiful Florida home. However, Dave's 401(k) represented the bulk of their assets, and they were counting on it for their retirement income. When they got married, they were very careful to update their wills and powers of attorney.

Then unexpectedly, Dave had a heart attack. To Carol's anguish, he passed quickly. Even though they had recently updated their important documents, it took some time for her to sort through their finances. She found that Dave had never changed the beneficiary on his 401(k). His prior wife was still the primary beneficiary. She was surprised but not overly concerned. The will had the correct information about who should get Dave's savings.

It wasn't until she tried to have the account switched over to her name that she found there was a problem. The beneficiary designation on a 401(k), IRA, or insurance contract overrides any other documentation when determining who will inherit the account. As the primary beneficiary, Dave's ex-wife was entitled to the full balance of his 401(k).

Carol went to Dave's ex-wife's home to speak to her, hoping to convince her to turn over the money out of a sense of fairness. Carol thought she had her sympathy, but in the end, Dave's ex-wife kept the money.

Carol was left to retire on only the small savings they had outside the 401(k) and Social Security. The situation was so heartrending she felt she couldn't even stay in Florida. She relocated, adding the proceeds from the sale of their home to her savings.

She built a new life for herself away from the painful memories. It was not the life she had planned. Not that it could be without Dave. But it could have been more comfortable had she inherited his retirement account as he'd intended.

get the money they need to raise them. Name your spouse, your children's guardian, or a family trust as the beneficiary instead.

For most accounts, it's easy to change your beneficiary. You can usually update your account online. Don't make a terrible mistake for your family simply because you didn't pay attention to this.

Trust for the Children

The cleanest solution for assuring that your children get the benefits of what you have set up for them in the event of your death is a **family trust**. This is a legal entity that can become the owner of your valuable assets. It allows your family to have access to your assets according to your will without going through **probate**. Probate is the legal process that validates your will (if you have one) and assures all your debts are settled and your remaining assets are distributed. Probate can take a year or more and cost up to 5 percent of the value of your assets.

With a family trust, all the assets whose titles have been transferred to the trust are freely accessible by the trustees and beneficiaries. You can designate the trust as the beneficiary of your retirement and insurance accounts, ensuring that the money is immediately available to those who will need it.

To establish a family trust, consult with an attorney. The cost for a family trust ranges depending on the complexity, but one can be prepared for about the same cost as a will. Especially if you have children, this extra step is well worth it.

The Rest of the Estate

While you are thinking about wills and trusts, it isn't a much bigger leap to a full estate plan. It will include documents that help your family make decisions and manage your affairs while you are alive if you have become incapacitated. These include a **health care directive**, a **medical power of attorney**, and a **financial power of attorney.**

A health care directive, or living will, documents your wishes regarding the types of care you want to receive. This may include how far you want medical personnel to go to keep you alive, the type of pain medications you wish to receive, and whether you prefer to spend your last days at home or in a hospital.

A medical power of attorney gives a person you name authority to make health care decisions for you in line with your wishes. A financial power of attorney gives a person you trust authorization to pay your bills and otherwise manage your affairs while you are incapacitated. These are separate documents, and you can name different people for each.

In addition to these legal documents, record your online accounts with your usernames and passwords, and save them in a safe place, such as a safe-deposit box. This is so the person who has your financial power of attorney knows what accounts you have and can easily access them.

Make sure that anyone who will be responsible for handling any of your affairs knows where all your important documents are located. You should walk them through your wishes so they will know what to expect if the need arises.

Long-Term Care

The costs of long-term care are nothing short of frightening. The Society of Actuaries estimates the average cost to care for an Alzheimer's patient, as an example, is $56,300 per year.[176] The National Association of Insurance Commissioners (NAIC) reports nationwide average nursing home costs run $78,000 per year and assisted living runs around $39,000 per year.[177]

One in nine people over the age of sixty-five in the United States has Alzheimer's, and more have other forms of dementia. Alzheimer's and dementia are just two of the many conditions that you will face as you get older that could leave you needing long-term care of some sort. About two-thirds of people over the age of sixty-five are expected to need long-term care in their lifetime.

How will you pay for these kinds of expenses? Medicare and Medicare Supplement policies do not cover the cost of long-term care, and neither does health insurance. Medicaid will cover the costs of nursing home care as well as some in-home and community-based services for low-income families with little to no savings. It will not cover the costs of assisted living or memory care facilities.

Medicaid pays for about two-thirds of all *paid* long-term services and support costs in the United States.[178] But most care is provided informally by family members and is paid for with individual savings and out of family members' income.

Long-term care insurance can help you pay for care not provided by Medicare or traditional health insurance. These policies reimburse you a daily amount (up to a preselected limit) for services to assist you with the activities of daily living, such as bathing, dressing, or eating. You can select a range of care options and benefits that allow you to get the services you need whether at home or in a facility.

Long-term care (LTC) insurance is worth considering for some. However, premiums for LTC are high. The average cost to cover a couple at age sixty is about $3,400 per year, with premiums rising for older ages. The NAIC recommends paying no more than 7 percent of your annual income in premiums. If your annual income is less than $49,000 per year, LTC insurance may be out of reach.[179]

LTC insurance may be a good option for you if you can afford the premiums and if spending down your assets to pay for care would put your partner in a difficult financial situation. The best time to buy LTC coverage is when you are between the ages of fifty-two and sixty-four. After that the premiums become even more costly.

In deciding whether you can afford the premiums, build in some room for future premium increases. While regulations require insurance companies to have rate increases approved by the state, LTC premiums have been known to rise by double digits. It would be a shame to allow your coverage to lapse because you can't afford it any longer.

Unfortunately, the market for LTC insurance is very thin. Ten insurance companies account for 78 percent of the market.[180] Before you buy, shop several carriers. Some states provide a summary of carriers offering policies in the state and include information on the company's financial strength and history of rate increases. If that isn't available in your state, ask your agent for the information.

There are alternatives to a strictly long-term care policy. Some whole life insurance and annuity policies provide benefits if you need long-term care. For example, some life insurance policies allow you to tap the death benefit while you are alive if you meet certain criteria for needing care, and some income annuities are designed to increase your monthly payment based on the same criteria. These options are attractive because they offer benefits beyond the LTC insurance. They may also be a good alternative for those who can't get LTC coverage due to health issues.

Of course, the decision doesn't have to be all or nothing. You could use LTC insurance, life insurance, and/or an annuity to cover part of the costs and rely on your savings and investments for the balance. The key is having a plan for how you will manage your or your partner's care as you age. The earlier you begin to think about it, the more options will be available to you.

Get Organized

You will do your family a huge favor by organizing your important documents. You want them to be able to locate the information they need to manage your affairs and carry out your wishes. Use the following list to help you gather your paperwork and determine what you still need to get done.

- Property titles (real estate, cars, etc.)
- Bank, brokerage, and mutual fund accounts, including usernames and passwords and beneficiaries for IRA accounts

- Work-related benefit plans such as life, health, and disability insurance, and retirement savings accounts, including the current beneficiary designations
- Private auto, homeowner, life, and disability insurance policies, including agent contact information
- Marriage certificates or divorce decrees
- Birth certificates
- Previous year's income tax returns
- Social Security number
- A list of debts, including the financial institution and payment due dates
- Military papers
- Any business agreements, like corporate, partnership, or sole proprietor business registrations
- Names and phone numbers of those to be notified if you are seriously ill or have passed away
- List of personal advisers, such as your financial planner, accountant, attorney, and doctor, including their contact information
- Last will and testament
- Family trust documents
- Medical care directive or living will
- Durable medical power of attorney
- Durable financial power of attorney

No one likes to think about dying or becoming disabled. However, as with saving, thinking about it early gives you many more options than if you put it off. Since you've worked so hard at your financial security, do your family the favor of preserving it when you are no longer able.

Vocabulary

Estate plan: All the documents and insurance that help your family carry out your wishes if you pass away or become incapacitated.

Term life insurance: Life insurance that lasts for a specific period, like ten or twenty years. The benefit will be paid if you die within that period. Premiums stay level. The policy can be canceled at any time.

Whole life insurance: Life insurance that lasts for your whole life—in other words, it is permanent. The benefit and premium are guaranteed for life. The policy develops a cash value that you can borrow against or withdraw. The death benefit is decreased by the cash value taken out.

Family trust: A legal entity that can own your valuable assets. Assets in a family trust are not subject to probate; therefore, your family can use them in accordance with your will immediately following your death. If you have children, a family trust is a good alternative as a beneficiary for your retirement and insurance accounts.

Probate: A legal process that validates your will, ensures your debts are paid, and distributes your remaining assets.

Health care directive or living will: A document establishing the type of medical care you want to receive in the event you cannot provide direction yourself.

Medical power of attorney: A document designating an individual to make medical decisions for you in alignment with your health care directive or your best interests if there is no health care directive.

Financial power of attorney: A document authorizing an individual to handle your financial affairs for you if you are unable to do it yourself.

Long-term care insurance: Insurance that helps pay for services Medicare and Medicaid do not, including in-home services, assisted living, nursing home care, and so on.

Main Ideas

1. Everyone needs a will. Regardless of how much you own or have saved, you want to control the distribution of your assets if you are no longer around. If you don't have a will, the state where you live will distribute your assets according to their rules, which may not match with your intentions.
2. You need life insurance when someone else is dependent on your income. As you get older and your savings grow, you need less life insurance. Because of the declining need for life insurance, term life insurance is adequate for most people.
3. Beneficiary designations determine what will happen with your retirement and insurance accounts regardless of what your will says. Update your beneficiaries whenever you have a life change.
4. Children under the age of eighteen should not be made beneficiaries. Financial institutions will not distribute money to a minor. Designate another family member, the children's guardian, or a family trust as the beneficiary instead.
5. Keep your important papers together in a safe location so your family members and those you have appointed to help can take care of your affairs more easily.

Chapter 13

How to Begin

BUILDING YOUR FINANCIAL SECURITY TAKES TIME AND DEDI-
cation. It is something you'll work on for the rest of your life. But
with such a large undertaking, where do you start? To conclude
our time together, you will lay the foundation and draw up your
own plans.

To help you see what you are trying to accomplish, you'll
work alongside a sample family, the Hartlands. Hal and Hannah
Hartland are in their early thirties, and they live with their three-
year-old, Haley. They are both professionals.

They believe they make a good income, but they don't understand why they can't get ahead. Their monthly bills keep them
from saving. They have no emergency fund and little in retirement
savings. They have $59,000 in debt over and above their mortgage,
$32,000 in student loans, and $27,000 in credit card and auto
loans. Follow Hal and Hannah's steps and use their templates to
help you get started on your own plan.

Week 1: Name Your Goals and Gather Your Information
The first step is to list your goals. They are the reason you save
money, after all. Make them compelling so you feel they are

worth working toward. To give them definition, you'll need to gather some information, but to start out, just list your current ones. The following are goals everyone should have. Add your unique goals to it.

Goals	
Protect against financial setbacks	Establish an emergency fund, eliminate nonmortgage debt, acquire disability insurance and property insurance
Retire by age _____	Contribute to employer retirement plan, individual retirement accounts, and additional savings as needed; eliminate all debt
Take care of family if I die or cannot speak for myself	Establish a will, life insurance, and/or family trust; manage beneficiary designations; create medical and financial powers of attorney and health care directive/living will
Other goals	Your unique financial goals

For now, Hal and Hannah's list looks like this:

Goals	
Protect against financial setbacks	Three months of expenses in an emergency fund Eliminate credit card, auto, and student loan debt Review disability insurance coverage
Retire by age 67	Invest in both 401(k) plans to get the match More savings later as it becomes possible

Goals	
Take care of family if I die or cannot speak for myself	Prepare a will and other necessary documents online Correct beneficiary designations Make sure life insurance is adequate
Send Haley to college	Invest in a 529 plan

Next, gather together your financial information. Look for the following documents and information:

- Current statements for your savings and investment accounts
- Current statements for your loans, including credit cards, student loans, your mortgage loan, and any other debt you may have
- A current or end-of-year pay stub
- The details of how you spent your money for the last several months from your bank and credit card companies if available; if not, begin tracking your spending from now forward
- All insurance policies you have, including your work-related health, life, and disability insurance, which will be available from your human resources department, plus any private life and disability insurance as well as your property insurance
- Any estate planning documents, including your will, family trust, health care directive, and powers of attorney if you have them

Once you have your documents together, make a list of your savings and investment accounts and their balances. Then list your loans, the current required payments, interest rates, and balances. While you're at it, you can also list the web addresses, usernames, and passwords. These will need to be saved in a secure place.

List your health care plan deductible and out-of-pocket maximum, the death benefit on your life insurance, and how much you would receive from any disability policies. List the beneficiaries of your retirement accounts and insurance policies. Hal and Hannah's list follows:

Account	Balance	Deposit/Payment
Hal's 401(k)	$5,674	$0
Hannah's 401(k)	$9,946	$0
Savings	$0	$0
Checking	$1,450	
Total savings	$17,070	
Mortgage 3.35%	$148,315	$791
Credit card 15.5%	$10,155	$140
Car loan 1 4.0%	$9,892	$218
Car loan 2 4.0%	$6,856	$155
Student loan 1 6.0%	$18,366	$355
Student loan 2 6.0%	$13,916	$183
Total debt	$207,500	$1,842

Account	Deductible/ Benefit	Out-of-Pocket Max	Beneficiary
Health insurance	$4,000	$12,000	
Life insurance Hal	$60,000		Hannah/Haley
Life insurance Hannah	$60,000		Hal/Haley
Disability insurance Hal	60% of income after 9 weeks		Hal
Disability insurance Hannah	60% of income after 9 weeks		Hannah
Car insurance	$1,000		
Homeowner's insurance	$1,000		

This is a good start. Now you know what you have, and it is all organized in one place. In the next week, you'll define and prioritize your goals.

Week 2: Define Your Goals

To change your goals from ideas into something you can work on, you need to put some numbers on them. If you need an emergency fund, how big should it be? If you need to save more for retirement, how much more? And so on. To do that, you must

first figure out how much you spend and where it is generally
going. Then you can put some specificity to your goals.

Gather as much information as you can about your spending.
If your bank or credit card companies have the tools, you may
be able to see their categorization of your expenses for several
months on their website. If not, you can likely come up with the
last month's detail from your latest statements. Then you can
begin tracking your spending for a more accurate picture going
forward. Keep a daily log or check register.

Hal and Hannah's credit card company does categorize their
expenses, so they were able to pull together some detail. They
can refine the categories going forward, but what they have gives
them enough to work with. The following table shows their average spending over six months by category. Add in your information alongside theirs.

Category		Hal & Hannah	You
Housing	Mortgage	$791	
	Taxes/ Insurance	$159	
	Gas	$34	
	Electricity	$65	
	Water/Sewer	$68	
Total housing		$1,117	
Childcare		$850	
Transportation	Car insurance	$192	

Category		Hal & Hannah	*You*
	Gas	$208	
Total transportation		*$400*	
Debt	Credit card	$140	
	Auto	$373	
	Student loans	$538	
Total nonmortgage debt		*$1,051*	
TV/Internet/Phone		$324	
Daily living	Groceries	$432	
	Clothing	$215	
	Restaurants	$409	
	Entertainment	$168	
	Other	$230	
Total daily living		*$1,454*	
Your other categories			
Total expenses		**$5,196**	
Monthly take-home pay		$5,235	

Hal and Hannah's situation is precarious. They are paying their bills, but just. A financial setback could have them losing their home, and their expenses over the last several months haven't included car or home repairs or health care. They need to shore up their financial security as quickly as possible.

Emergency Fund

The Hartlands' first goal, as is yours, is to create a financial cushion in the form of an emergency fund. You should be able to cover your expenses for at least three months. You could simply take your total expenses and multiply them by three to come up with a goal for your cushion. In Hal and Hannah's case, that total would be about $15,000. It would give them much more security, but it's more than they need to start with.

Your emergency fund can be based on just your mandatory expenses for housing, debt, groceries, and the like. After all, in the worst case, you'll cut out your discretionary expenses. Hal and Hannah's mandatory expenses are summarized in the following table. The grocery number has been increased to account for more meals at home and no meals at restaurants.

Mandatory Expenses	Hal & Hannah	*You*
Housing	$1,117	
Childcare	$850	
Transportation	$400	
Debt	$1,051	

Mandatory Expenses	Hal & Hannah	*You*
Groceries	$630	
Total	$4,048	

As discussed in chapter 8, your emergency fund is primarily there to help you cover expenses in the event you can't bring in an income for a short time. You can get away with assuming you and your partner won't be out of work at the same time, so your emergency fund only needs to cover one of your incomes. For the worst-case scenario, assume you lose the biggest one. In the following table, Hal and Hannah assume they lose Hannah's pay, which is bigger, leaving them to live on only Hal's pay.

Monthly Income	Hal & Hannah	*You*
Total household income	$5,235	
Lowest income	$2,500	
Assumed income lost	$2,735	

Since Hal's pay won't be enough to cover their mandatory expenses, the shortfall between the two is what they need to make up. Subtract your remaining income from your mandatory expenses to come up with the monthly shortfall and multiply by the number of months you want to cover. Hal and Hannah will start with the minimum of three months of expenses, which would total about $4,600.

Emergency Fund	Hal & Hannah	*You*
A. Mandatory expenses	$4,048	
B. Remaining income	$2,500	
C. Monthly shortfall (A – B)	$1,548	
D. Minimum emergency fund (C × 3)	**$4,644**	

Company Match in Your Retirement Savings Plan

Once your emergency fund is in place, the next priority is to contribute enough to your retirement savings plan to get your full company match if your company offers one. The reason this is the next important goal is because it's free money. If you don't go for the match, it's like saying you want a pay cut. Retirement savings plans were covered in chapter 9.

Determine what the company match is from the plan website or your human resources department and then how much you need to contribute. The match is normally stated as a percentage of your pay. Multiply that by your pay before taxes and any other deductions in one pay period to come up with your contribution goal.

Hal and Hannah's goal for their monthly retirement plan contributions after they have saved up their emergency fund follows:

	Hal	Hannah	Total
A. Gross pay (before taxes and benefits)	$3,164	$4,315	$7,479
B. Company match formula	5%	5%	5%

	Hal	Hannah	Total
H&H contribution goal (A × B)	$158.20	$215.75	$373.95
Company contribution (A × B)	$158.20	$215.75	$373.95
Total contribution	$316.40	$431.50	$747.90

Get Out of Debt

If you have debt other than your mortgage, once you are getting your full company match in your retirement account, your next goal is to pay that off. Decide which loans you should work on first, using either a debt snowball or debt avalanche approach from chapter 7. Making only the minimum payments on your other loans, write down how much extra you could pay on the loan on which you will focus first. Here are Hal and Hannah's from week one.

Loan	Balance	Minimum Payment	Extra Payment	Total Payment
Car loan 2 4.0%	$6,856	$155	$100	$255
Car loan 1 4.0%	$9,892	$218		$218
Credit card 15.5%	$10,155	$140		$140
Student loan 2 6.0%	$13,916	$183		$183

Loan	Balance	Minimum Payment	Extra Payment	Total Payment
Student loan 1 6.0%	$18,366	$355		$355
Total	$59,185	$1,051		$1,151

Determine whether you will have other sources of money, besides your regular pay, to add to your progress on these goals. If you are expecting to get a tax refund or a bonus, decide now that it will be used to bolster your emergency fund or pay down debt. Hal and Hannah don't have any other sources of income right now.

Long-Term Goals

If you are working on these first three goals, define your other goals in broad terms. Put a dollar value on them now if you can. If not, you can do that later.

However, if you have accomplished getting out of debt, it is time to get serious about saving for retirement. If you can't meet your target right away, decide on a path forward. For example, decide to put future pay increases toward retirement savings.

For Hal and Hannah, it's a little early to put a fine point on their ultimate monthly retirement savings target. It will take them a few years to get out of debt. But a ballpark total savings number based on their current expenses is possible.

Taking out their debt payments, which will be gone long before they retire, their monthly spending would be $3,395. Using the rule of thumb of $333 of monthly spending per $100,000 saved from chapter 4, they'll need at least $1 million by the time they do retire. From the table on page 79 in chapter 4, their minimum target savings per month over 30 years will be $820. With their savings to get their company match as well as their companies' contributions, they will already be setting aside $748 per month. So they will need to save an additional $72.

	Hal & Hannah	*You*
A. Monthly spending	$5,235	
B. Debt payments	$1,842	
C. Spending w/o debt (A – B)	$3,393	
D. Multiple of $100,000 needed (C ÷ 333)	10.2	
E. Total savings needed	≈$1 million	
F. Monthly savings needed (table in chapter 4)	$820	
G. Total savings with company match (from long-term goals section of this chapter)	$748	
H. Additional savings needed (F – G)	$72	

They will ultimately need to fine-tune their number. Income they receive after they retire, like Social Security benefits, isn't included in this rough estimate. Their spending will change as they work toward their goals, and the cost of maintaining their lifestyle will naturally rise over time. The investment returns they earn will fluctuate. Hal and Hannah will need to recalculate their required savings regularly, but once the debt is paid off, they will have the flexibility to save more.

Hal and Hannah also want to send Haley to college. Given their current situation, they have some work to do before they can work that goal into their plans. Once they are in a less precarious position, they can decide how to approach it. One possibility would be to put what they are spending on daycare into college savings once Haley is in school.

You may be able to work on multiple goals at once. List as many goals as you can with as much definition as you have. Don't forget about the administrative goals, like putting an estate plan in place, reviewing your insurance and investments, or finding an adviser.

These are the administrative goals Hal and Hannah want to work on:

- Review beneficiary designations.
- Look into an online legal service provider to prepare a will, a health care directive, and medical and financial powers of attorney.
- Make an appointment with insurance agent to review life insurance.

Fortunately, they already have disability insurance through work, so they won't need to acquire that, though in the future they may want to add to it. They will need to correct their beneficiaries on their life insurance policies and retirement accounts. They have listed Haley as a secondary beneficiary after each other. Haley will not be able to receive a retirement plan distribution or life insurance proceeds until she turns eighteen. Since the couple is planning to have Hannah's parents raise Haley if they both perish, Hannah's parents are good candidates for the secondary beneficiary designation.

This week was all about defining your goals. For Hal and Hannah, it's hard to see how they will meet theirs at this point; however, with some changes to their spending habits, it is possible. Now that you have your goals, the next week is dedicated to figuring out how to achieve them.

Week 3: Develop Your Strategy

If you are like Hal and Hannah, you won't be able to simply save more. You probably need to figure out where you can spend less first. Hal and Hannah won't be able to accomplish everything at once, and neither will you. Instead take it one step at a time.

Step 1: Forecast Future Expenses

The information you gathered in the last week is a good start, but it doesn't capture all your spending. You still need to estimate the cost of future expenses like home or car maintenance, health care costs, and other spending you can predict. Hal and Hannah will be adding the following expenses to their monthly spending plan.

- Car maintenance and repairs: $250
- Home maintenance and repairs: $100
- Health care: $100
- Holidays/birthdays: $25

The couple needs to carve out space in their budget for a total of $475 in additional untracked expenses. They will incur them eventually even though they haven't in the last six months. The reason the couple is frustrated with their finances is they are spending all their money without taking these inevitable costs into account.

Step 2: Strategy to Cut Spending to Raise an Emergency Fund

To create space for their goals and the $475 in untracked expenses, they will need to cut back somewhere. Prime categories for savings are discretionary expenses. Hal and Hannah agreed to make the following changes in their spending temporarily so they can raise their emergency fund as quickly as possible.

- Get rid of cable television. They will have internet and cell phone service only. Financial security is more important than 150 TV channels they don't have time to watch anyway.
- Avoid buying clothes until the emergency fund is in place. Hal and Hannah have plenty, and Haley's cousins will provide hand-me-downs.
- Avoid going to restaurants. All meals will be prepared at home at least until the emergency fund is in place.
- No spending dumped into the "other" category. They will identify where every dollar is spent.

Category	Average Expense	Planned Expense	Saved
TV/internet/phone	$324	$120	$204
Clothing	$215	$0	$215
Restaurants	$409	$0	$409
Additional groceries	$432	$630	($198)

Category	Average Expense	Planned Expense	Saved
Entertainment	$168	$50	$118
Other	$230	$0	$230
Total	**$1,778**	**$800**	**$978**

They've identified $978 in possible savings. After the additional $475 of future expenses, Hal and Hannah have $503 to apply to their goal of building an emergency fund. It will take them nine months to raise the $4,600 in their goal. Along the way, they will have also saved $4,275 toward car and home maintenance, health care, and holidays and birthdays. As these expenses come up, they will have money set aside to pay for them without depleting their emergency fund or adding to their debt.

Step 3: Strategy to Contribute to Retirement Plans to Get the Company Match

Once Hal and Hannah's emergency fund is saved, that monthly savings can be put toward contributing to their 401(k)s to get their company matches. They must contribute $374 to get the full match.

If they contribute to a Roth account, the full $374 will come out of their pay, leaving them $129 to put toward paying down their debt and other expenses. The advantage of a Roth account is that future withdrawals are fully tax-free. See chapter 9 for more details.

Alternatively, they could decide to contribute to a traditional account for the time being to get the full match with a discount from the tax benefit. Their pretax contribution of $374 would only reduce their take-home pay by $296. Most retirement websites have a calculator to help you figure out your take-home pay after a contribution. If your plan does not have one, go to www.dinkytown.net and click "Retirement Savings & Planning" under "Calculators." Hal and Hannah will have to pay taxes on their withdrawals in the future, but the current tax break makes it easier to save what they need to now.

Since their debt payments are making saving difficult and their expense reduction efforts to raise their emergency fund were draconian, they decided to contribute to a traditional account. That lets them meet their extra debt payment goal of $100 and have a little left over to add a few extras they have been missing. Once they have more flexibility, they can choose to change future retirement contributions to a Roth account if they want. The following table shows their new budget. The items in bold are those that have changed.

Category		Old	New
Housing	Mortgage	$791	$791
	Taxes/insurance	$159	$159
	Gas	$34	$34
	Maintenance/repairs	**$0**	**$100**
	Electricity	$65	$65
	Water/Sewer	$68	$68
Total housing		*$1,117*	*$1,217*

Category		Old	New
Childcare		$850	$850
Transportation	Car insurance	$192	$192
	Car repair and maintenance	**$0**	**$250**
	Gas	$208	$208
Total transportation		*$400*	*$650*
Debt	Credit card	$140	$140
	Auto	$373	$373
	Student loans	$538	$538
Total nonmort-gage debt		*$1,051*	*$1,051*
TV/internet/phone		$324	$120
Daily living	**Groceries**	$432	$630
	Clothing	$215	$45
	Restaurants	$409	$80
	Entertainment	$168	$50
	Other	$230	$0
Total daily living		*$1,454*	*$805*

Category		Old	New
Health care		$0	$100
Holidays/ birthdays		$0	$46
Total expenses		$5,194	$4,839
Retirement savings		$0	$296
Extra debt payment		$0	$100
Total expenses/ savings		$0	$5,235
Monthly take-home pay		$5,235	$5,235

Step 4: Strategy to Pay Off Debt

Hal and Hannah have budgeted an extra $100 per month for debt payments. They will use a debt snowball approach, shown in chapter 7, to pay off all their debt except their mortgage. They will add $100 to their smallest loan, and when that is paid off, they will add the payment they were making on that loan to the payment they are making to the next one in line. They'll keep doing that until all the loans are paid off.

With an extra payment of $100 per month applied to their smallest car loan, Hal and Hannah will be able to pay off that car in twenty-five months. That will free up $255 from their budget.

Because they need more life insurance, they will use $100 of the extra money each month to add $500,000 in term life insurance for each of them. They will adjust their budget accordingly when the time comes. The remaining $155 will be put toward an extra payment on their second car loan.

They plan to use the full amount freed from paying off each of the remaining loans to pay extra on the next loan in line. The final loan—student loan two—will be paid off over its normal term at the same time student loan one is paid off. You can see how quickly you can get out of debt with an online debt snowball calculator such as the one provided by the Financial Mentor website. The table on the next pages shows Hal and Hannah's debt snowball.

In four years and seven months, Hal and Hannah will have raised an emergency fund, saved money for foreseeable expenses, added life insurance, and paid off all their debt other than their mortgage. With their nonmortgage debt paid off, they will have an extra $1,051 available in their monthly budget.

The extra money is more than enough to meet their full minimum retirement savings target, and they can add to that number. It will also allow them to save for things like the replacements for their current cars, keeping them out of debt in the future. They will have much more flexibility and security.

This detailed strategy allows the Hartlands to see their path forward. Yes, it will take some time to work through their first few goals, but they know what they have to do. They may not follow the strategy exactly. Along the way they can make changes. They are likely to see pay increases. They could see setbacks. The beauty is that they will know how the changes affect their goals. Their decisions will be fully informed and based on their priorities.

Now you can create your own strategy.

Loans	Balance	Minimum Payment	Extra Payment
Car loan 1	$6,856	$155	$100
Car loan 1 paid off. Use extra $155 of the total to increase payment on car loan 2.			
Car loan 2	$9,892	$218	$155
Car loan 2 paid off. Use extra $373 to increase payment on credit card.			
Credit card	$10,155	$140	$373
Credit card paid off. Use extra $513 to increase payment on student loan 1.			
Student loan 1	$13,916	$183	$513
Student loan 1 paid off. Student loan 2 paid off over contract term.			
Student loan 2	$18,367	$355	$0

- Prepare a budget that incorporates your normal monthly expenses and an allocation for predictable future expenses. Whittle down your expenses so you have money to put toward your first goal.
- Assign every dollar a job. If it is not going toward a current or future expense, it should be going toward your debt reduction or savings goals.
- Map out a path to achieving your top priority goals. If you can't work on all your goals at once, attack the first one and estimate when and how you will work on the next one.

Loans	Total Payment	Beginning	Ending
Car Loan 1	$255	9 months	34 months
Car Loan 2	$373	34 months	44 months
Credit Card	$513	44 months	52 months
Student loan 1	$696	52 months	55 months
Student loan 2	$355	No change	55 months

Do as much as you can. Even small amounts count. As you learn how to pay attention to your spending and prioritize your goals, you will be able to do more.

Week 4: Open Accounts

You've done the hard work of identifying your goals, assessing your situation, and creating a strategy. Now it's time to open the accounts you need to get started.

- Open a savings account for your emergency fund and those future expenses that don't come up every month. Decide if you need separate accounts or if you can keep track of what you have in each category another way.

- You may be able to save for health care expenses in a health savings account with tax benefits. Sign up if so.
- Automate as much of your saving as possible. With most employers, you can have money direct deposited to multiple accounts. Begin a direct deposit of your target savings.
- Sign up for your company 401(k) if you haven't already. Choose a target-date retirement fund, or a managed account to start with if one is available. You can make changes later if you want to do more of your own investment decision-making. For now, you just want to start contributing.
- Check with your human resources department about whether disability insurance is available and, if so, what is covered. Sign up.
- If you're maxing out your retirement plan or you don't have one through work, open an IRA with a discount broker or mutual fund company.
- Start the process to consolidate as many of your accounts as possible with one financial institution. Do you have old 401(k) accounts from prior employers? Roll them into your current 401(k) or a rollover IRA account.
- Make changes to your beneficiaries as needed.
- Make an appointment with your insurance agent for a review of your coverage. Add to your property, disability, and life insurance as needed.
- Sign up for an online legal service, like Rocket Lawyer or LegalZoom, or find an estate planning attorney. Start working on the documents your family will need to handle your affairs if something terrible happens to you.

Month 2: Review

You are off and running. The remaining challenge is to stay on track. To make progress on your goals, you must know whether your efforts are paying off. A regular review is an important part of meeting your goals. Seeing the small successes will also help motivate you to keep going.

- Review your actual spending against your budget, and determine if you need to adjust the budget based on what you learned. You may need to refine your budget for a couple of months before you get it right, but eventually it will be stable.
- Verify that your intended deposits have begun.
- Make sure your 401(k) contributions are what you expected and you are getting the company match. Check that your money is going into the correct investment.
- Follow up if anything is not going according to plan.

Ongoing Reviews

Your financial security will always require your attention. As you develop saving habits, you may need to spend less time on it on a day-to-day basis, but it's important to review your progress regularly.

- Review your short-term savings and debt balances quarterly to see if you are on track. If not, decide what needs to change.
- Review your long-term savings targets and balances, like retirement or college savings, annually.
- Review your investments at least annually and rebalance your strategy if necessary.
- If you are using a target-date retirement fund, rebalancing isn't required, nor is it with a managed account, robo-, or

human adviser. It will be taken care of for you. However, it is important to revisit the assumptions the manager or your adviser have for you annually, since changes in your circumstances may affect your investment strategy.

- Review your beneficiary designations and insurance needs annually. If you have a life change, review them immediately.

- Review your goals annually. Your goals will change. You may decide to take your life in a different direction. You may need more or less money to fulfill your goals. Whatever way your goals change, the progress you've made on your old goals will help you reach your new ones.

- Review your will, trusts, and other documents every three to five years, or as changing circumstances would dictate. Even if you have no changes, it's good to refresh your memory about your intentions.

With a regular review, you can adjust your strategy as needed. Don't forget to celebrate your accomplishments. Managing your budget and reaching your short-term savings goals are just as worthy as reaching long-term savings milestones.

Financial security is not something that can only be had by a few lucky people. It is something you can build for yourself. It takes knowing what is necessary and diligently working on it every month. You must decide what is important to you and what is not. And you must live those values every day and with every big decision. Wherever you are, you can take the steps to have a comfortable lifestyle that is insulated from setbacks for the rest of your life. Decide today to save yourself.

Endnotes

Introduction

1. Huddleston, "69% of Americans Have Less than $1,000 in Savings."

2. Vanguard, "How America Saves 2017: Vanguard 2016 Defined Contribution Plan Data."

3. El Issa, "NerdWallet's 2017 American Household Credit Card Debt Study."

Chapter 1

4. Hirshbein, "William Osler and *The Fixed Period*."

5. Schieber, *The Predictable Surprise*, 24.

6. Weaver, "Support of the Elderly before the Depression," 509, Table-1.

7. Schieber, *The Predictable Surprise*, 29.

8. Schieber, *The Predictable Surprise*, 34.

9. Schieber, *The Predictable Surprise*, 132.

10. Skolnik, "Private Pension Plans," 4.

11. DeNavas-Walt and Proctor, *Income and Poverty in the United States*, 14.

12. Schieber, *The Predictable Surprise*, 160.

13. Schieber, *The Predictable Surprise*, 157, 158.

14. Wiatrowski, "The Last Private Industry Pension Plans," 3–18.

15. Farnham, "Public Pensions Face Underfunding Crisis."

16. Social Security and Medicare Boards of Trustees, "A Summary of the 2015 Annual Reports."

17. Schieber, *The Predictable Surprise*, 38–40.

18. Schieber, *The Predictable Surprise*, 76–84.

19. Social Security and Medicare Boards of Trustees, "A Summary of the 2015 Annual Reports."

20. Social Security and Medicare Boards of Trustees, "A Summary of the 2015 Annual Reports."

21. US Bureau of Economic Analysis, *National Economic Accounts.*

22. Employee Benefit Research Institute, "Retirement Income Adequacy."

23. Cubanski et al., "How Many Seniors Are Living in Poverty?"

24. Cubanski et al., "How Many Seniors Are Living in Poverty?"

25. Organisation for Economic Co-operation and Development, "Better Life Index—United States."

26. Social Security Administration, "Benefits Planner: Life Expectancy."

27. US Bureau of Labor Statistics, "Civilian Labor Force Participation Rate by Age, Sex, Race, and Ethnicity."

28. Rho, *Hard Work?*, 1.

29. US Bureau of Labor Statistics, "Employment status of the civilian noninstitutional population by disability status and age, 2016 and 2017 annual averages." The number of individuals not in the labor force and over the age of 64 with a disability divided by the totoal number of individuals over the age of 64 who are not in the workforce.

30. DePillis, "Why Age Discrimination Is Worse for Women."

31. Taylor, *The Return of the Multi-Generational Household*, 1.

Chapter 2

32. Thaler and Sunstein, *Nudge*, 73.

33. Hershfield et al., "Increased Saving Behavior through Age," 9.

34. Hershfield et al., "Increased Saving Behavior through Age," 7.

35. Hershfield et al., "Don't Stop Thinking about Tomorrow," 281–84.

36. Hershfield et al., "Increased Saving Behavior through Age," 27.

37. Scitovsky, *The Joyless Economy*, Kindle edition, loc. 479.

38. Statistic Brain, "Self Storage Industry Statistics."

39. Schwartz, *The Paradox of Choice.*

40. Steindl-Rast, "Want to Be Happy? Be Grateful."

41. Ecole Polytechnique Fédérale de Lausanne, "How Stress Tears Us Apart."

42. O'Connor, *Rewire*, 8–9.

43. Duhigg, *The Power of Habit*, Kindle edition, loc. 418–24.

44. Schwartz, *The Paradox of Choice*, 183.

45. Schwartz, *The Paradox of Choice*, 190.

46. HomeAdvisor, "How Much Does It Cost to Remodel a Kitchen?"

47. PureWow, "How Realistic Are TV Characters' New York Apartments?"

48. Taylor, "5 Things Home Improvement Reality TV Shows Don't Tell You."

49. Rogers et al., "Beyond Good Intentions," 33.

50. Canova and Manganelli Rattazzi, "Personality, Past Behaviour and Saving Intention," 9–10.

51. Lunt and Livingstone, "Psychological, Social and Economic Determinants of Saving," 621–41.

52. Sanburn, "So...Where'd All That Money Go?"

53. Page, "They Ain't Got No Money in the Bank."

54. Sass and Ramos-Mercado, *Are Americans of All Ages and Incomes Shortsighted about Their Finances?*, 4.

55. Woolley, "How a Harvard Economist Screwed Up—and Then Saved—Her Retirement."

56. U.S. Bank, *2016 U.S. Bank Parent Financial Survey.*

57. Council for Economic Education, *Survey of the States.*

58. FINRA Investor Education Foundation, *Financial Capability in the United States*, 32.

59. FINRA Investor Education Foundation, *Financial Capability in the United States*, 28.

60. FINRA Investor Education Foundation, *Financial Capability in the United States*, 13, 21.

61. McKeon, *Effective Sex Education.*

62. Thaler and Sunstein, *Nudge*, 74–75.

63. Roberts, "The Chinese Can't Kick Their Savings Habit."

64. Organisation for Economic Co-operation and Development, "Household Savings Forecasts" (1993–2017).

65. Börsch-Supan and Wilke, "The German Public Pension System."

66. US Bureau of Economic Analysis, "Personal Savings as a Percent of Disposable Income."

67. Clingman, Burkhalter, and Chaplan, "Replacement Rates for Hypothetical Retired Workers," 9.

68. Ortman, Velkoff, and Hogan, *An Aging Nation*, 2.

Chapter 3
69. Helman, Copeland, and VanDerhei, "The 2015 Retirement Confidence Survey," 1–36.

70. Peckham, *Physician Debt and Net Worth Report.*

71. Stanley and Danko, *The Millionaire Next Door*, Kindle edition, loc. 1919–27.

72. Helman, Copeland, and VanDerhei, "The 2015 Retirement Confidence Survey," 16.

73. Wolff and Gittleman, "Inheritances and the Distribution of Wealth," 22.

74. Gist and Figueiredo, "In Their Dreams," 4–6.

75. Social Security Administration, "Actuarial Life Table."

76. Consumer Financial Protection Bureau, *Snapshot of Older Consumers and Mortgage Debt.*

77. Cubanski et al., "How Much Is Enough?"

78. Greeley, "U.S. Homeowners Are Repeating Their Mistakes."

79. VanDerhei, "How Does the Probability of a 'Successful' Retirement Differ," 9.

80. T. Rowe Price, *First Look: Assessing the New Retiree Experience.*

81. Value Penguin, "Average Auto Loan Interest Rates."

82. Ma et al., *Trends in College Pricing.*

83. The Institute for College Access and Success, "Project on Student Debt."

84. US Department of Education, "Income-Driven Plans."

85. Sallie Mae, "How America Saves for College."

86. Ma et al., *Trends in College Pricing.*

87. DeNavas-Walt and Proctor, *Income and Poverty in the United States.*

88. Dr. Amy K. Glasmeier and MIT, Living Wage Calculator, created in 2014, revised in 2018, http://livingwage.mit.edu/.

89. US Census Bureau, *Selected Characteristics of Households by Total Money Income: 2014.*

Chapter 4

90. McCurry, "Early Retirement at 33."

91. Jacobson, "Start Here."

92. Economides and Economides, *America's Cheapest Family Gets You Right on the Money*, Kindle edition, loc. 264–641.

93. Scott, "The 50 Greatest Yogi Berra Quotes."

94. Eisenberg, *The Number*, Kindle edition, loc. 680–89.

95. Bengen, "How Much Is Enough?," 1–9.

96. Clingman, Burkhalter, and Chaplain, "Replacement Rates for Hypothetical Retired Workers," 9.

Chapter 5

97. "How Mint Works," Mint, accessed November 2017, https://www.mint.com/how-mint-works.

98. "Pricing," YNAB, accessed October 8, 2018, https://www.youneedabudget.com/pricing/.

99. Robinson, "Success of Auto Enrollment and Auto Increase."

100. Dworak-Fisher, "Access to Specific Provision of Employer Provided Benefits."

Chapter 6

101. Statistic Brain, "Gym Membership Market Analysis."

102. Internal Revenue Service, "Filing Season Statistics."

103. US Department of Agriculture, "Food Prices and Spending."

104. US Bureau of Labor Statistics, "Consumer Expenditures—2016."

105. Zagat, "The State of American Dining in 2015."

106. Gilbride, Inman, and Stilley, *What Determines Unplanned Purchases?*

107. Gunders, *Wasted*, 12.

108. Marum, "We Compared Prices at 7 Different Grocery Stores."

109. Rocha, *Pocket Your Dollars*, Kindle edition, loc. 2315–22.

110. Bankrate.com, "True Cost of Not Maintaining Your Car."

111. US Bureau of Labor Statistics, "Consumer Expenditures—2016."

112. American Public Transportation Association, "August Transit Savings Report."

Chapter 7

113. BankRate.com, "Current Mortgage Rates."

114. Consumer Financial Protection Bureau, "What Is a Debt-to-Income Ratio?"

115. Lewerer, "Car Depreciation."

116. Consumer Reports, "Make Your Car Last 200,000 Miles."

117. US Department of Transportation, "Average Annual Miles per Driver by Age Group."

118. Wolff-Mann, "The Average American Is in Credit Card Debt."

119. El Issa, "NerdWallet's 2017 American Household Credit Card Debt Study."

120. Queen, "Minimum Payment Survey."

121. National Bureau of Economic Research, "Borrowing from 401(k)s."

122. TIAA-Cref, *Are Your Employees Borrowing from Their Futures?*

123. Vilorio, "Data on Display."

124. The Institute for College Access and Success, "State Summary."

125. Brown et al., *Financial Education and the Debt Behavior of the Young.*

126. Schmeiser, Stoddard, and Urban, "Does Salient Financial Information Affect Academic Performance and Borrowing Behavior among College Students?"

127. Federal Student Aid, "Repayment Plans."

128. Consumer Financial Protection Bureau, "CFPB Finds Percentage of Borrowers with $20k in Student Debt Doubled over the Last Decade."

129. Dale and Krueger, "Estimating the Payoff to Attending a More Selective College."

130. Edvisors, "Interest Rates and Fees on Federal Student Loans."

Chapter 8

131. FINRA Investor Education Foundation, "Finanical Capability in the United States."

132. US Bureau of Labor Statistics, "Employment, Hours, and Earnings"; Challenger, Gray & Christmas Inc., "2016 December Job Cut Report."

133. Council for Disability Awareness, "Chances of Disability."

134. US Bureau of Labor Statistics, "Workers with Disability Insurance Plans."

135. Social Security Administration, "Benefit Calculations, Social Security Quick Calculator."

136. Council for Disability Awareness, "Chances of Disability."

137. Miller, "The Divorce Surge Is Over, but the Myth Lives On."

138. Magloff, "The Average Cost for Divorce."

Chapter 9

139. Graves, "2018 ACA Out-of-Pocket Maximums and Health Savings Account Limits."

140. Financial Engines, *Missing Out*.

141. Aon Hewitt, *Roth Usage in Defined Contribution Plans*.

142. Internal Revenue Service, "Publication 590-B."

143. Mackenzie, "Determining Whether 401(k) Plan Fees Are Reasonable."

144. Collins et al., "The Economics of Providing 401(k) Plans."

145. Collins et al., "The Economics of Providing 401(k) Plans."

146. The Pew Charitable Trusts, "Who's In, Who's Out."

147. Saving for College, "Name the Top 7 Benefits of 529 Plans."

148. Doyle, "How Often Do People Change Jobs?"

Chapter 10

149. Krejca, "How Many Stocks Make Up a Well-Diversified Portfolio?"

150. Investment Company Institute, *2017 Investment Company Fact Book*.

151. Investment Company Institute, *2017 Investment Company Fact Book*.

152. Morningstar, *The Morningstar Category Classifications*.

153. Kinnel, *Predictive Power of Fees*.

154. Vanguard, "Vanguard 500 Index Fund Investor Shares (VFINX)"; Vanguard, "Vanguard 500 Admiral Shares VFIAX."

155. Vanguard, "Vanguard S&P 500 Index ETF."

156. Charles Schwab, "Commissions & Trades."

157. Maye, "Average Investor 20 Year Return Astoundingly Awful."

158. MFS Fund Distributors Inc., "Emotion Drives Investor Decisions."

159. Tuchman, "Burt Malkiel on Active Management's Big Miss."

Chapter 11

160. Target Date Analytics, "A Brief History of Target Date Funds."

161. Munnell et al., "Investment Returns Defined Benefit vs Defined Contribution Plans". 4

162. VanDerhei et al., "401(k) Plan Asset Allocation, Account Balances, and Loan Activity in 2014."

163. Charlson et al., *Target-Date Series Research Paper.*

164. Charlson et al., *Target-Date Series Research Paper.*

165. Charlson et al., *Target-Date Series Research Paper.*

166. Kilroy, "Target-Date-Fund Fees Fall for Ninth Consecutive Year."

167. Bengen, "How Much Is Enough?"

168. "Our History," Financial Engines, accessed February 3, 2017, https://financialengines.com/about-us/history.

169. Steyer, "Cost, Complexity Cited for Lackluster Use of Managed Accounts."

170. FPA Research and Practice Institute, *Financial Planning in 2015*, 22-24."

171. FPA Research and Practice Institute, *Financial Planning in 2015*, 22-24.

Chapter 12

172. Jones, "Majority in U.S. Do Not Have a Will."

173. Dahl et al., "The Shocking Statistics Behind the Life Insurance Coverage Gap".

174. Federal Student Aid, "Dischard Due to Deat."

175. Saving for College, "Does a 529 Plan Affect Financial Aid?"

176. Rubin et al., *An Overview of the U.S. Long-Term Care Insurance Market*, 5.

177. National Association of Insurance Commissioners, *A Shopper's Guide to Long-Term Care Insurance.*

178. The SCAN Foundation, *Who Pays for Long-Term Care in the US?*

179. National Assoication of Insurance Commissioners, *A Shopper's Guide to Long-Term Care Insurance.*

180. Johnson, "Financing questions Loom as Private LTC Insurers Falter."

Bibliography

AAA. *Your Driving Costs.* Heathrow, FL: AAA Association Communication, 2016. https://publicaffairsresources.aaa.biz/wp-content/uploads/2016/03/2016-YDC-Brochure.pdf.

Advisory HQ. "Average Financial Advisor Fees & Costs: 2017–2018 Report." January 23, 2017. http://www.advisoryhq.com/articles/financial-advisor-fees-wealth-managers-planners-and-fee-only-advisors/.

American Public Transportation Association. "August Transit Savings Report." August 18, 2016. http://www.apta.com/mediacenter/pressreleases/2016/Pages/Transit-Savings.aspx.

Aon Hewitt. *Roth Usage in Defined Contribution Plans.* April 2014. http://www.aon.com/attachments/human-capital-consulting/2014_Roth-Usage-Defined-Contribution_Whitepaper_Final_April.pdf.

Bankrate.com. "Current Mortgage Rates—Mortgage Interest Rates Today." Accessed August 30, 2017. http://www.bankrate.com/finance/mortgages/current-interest-rates.aspx.

———. "True Cost of Not Maintaining Your Car." March 5, 2014. https://www.foxbusiness.com/features/true-cost-of-not-maintaining-your-car.

Bengen, Bill. "How Much Is Enough?" *Financial Advisor,* May 1, 2012. https://www.fa-mag.com/news/how-much-is-enough-10496.html.

Börsch-Supan, Axel, and Christina B. Wilke. "The German Public Pension System: How It Was, How It Will Be." Working paper, National Bureau of Economic Research, Cambridge, MA, May 2004. http://www.nber.org/papers/w10525.pdf.

Brown, Meta, John Grigsby, Wilbert van der Klaauw, Jaya Wen, and Basit Zafar. *Financial Education and the Debt Behavior of the Young.* Staff report no. 634.

September 2013, revised September 2015. https://www.newyorkfed.org
/medialibrary/media/research/staff_reports/sr634.pdf.

Canova, Luigina, and Anna Maria Manganelli Rattazzi. "Personality, Past
Behaviour and Saving Intention: A Test of an Extended Model of the Theory
of Planned Behaviour."

Charlson, Josh, Laura Pavlenko Lutton, David Falkof, Kailin Liu, Kathryn Spica,
and Janet Yang. *Target-Date Series Research Paper: 2013 Survey.* Morningstar
Fund Research. 2013. http://corporate.morningstar.com/us/documents
/ResearchPapers/2013TargetDate.pdf.

Challenger, Gray & Christmas Inc. "2016 December Job Cut Report: 33,627
Rounds Out Year of Low Job Cuts." January 5, 2017. https://www.chall
engergray.com/press/press-releases/2016-december-job-cut-report-33627
-rounds-out-year-low-job-cuts.

Charles Schwab. "Commissions & Trades." Accessed March 10, 2017.
http://www.schwab.com/public/schwab/investing/pricing_services
/fees_minimums.

Clingman, Michael, Kyle Burkhalter, and Chris Chaplan. "Replacement Rates
for Hypothetical Retired Workers." Actuarial Note Number 2014.9. Baltimore,
MD: Social Security Administration, Office of the Chief Actuary, 2014.

Collins, Sean, Sarah Holden, James Duvall, and Elena Barone Chism. "The
Economics of Providing 401(k) Plans: Services, Fees and Expenses, 2015." *ICI
Research Perspective* 22, no. 4 (2016). https://www.ici.org/pdf/per22-04.pdf.

Consumer Financial Protection Bureau. "CFPB Finds Percentage of Borrowers
with $20K in Student Debt Doubled over Last Decade." Press release. August
16, 2017. https://www.consumerfinance.gov/about-us/newsroom/cfpb
-finds-percentage-borrowers-20k-student-debt-doubled-over-last-decade/.

———. *Snapshot of Older Consumers and Mortgage Debt.* May 2014. http://files
.consumerfinance.gov/f/201405_cfpb_snapshot_older-consumers-mort
gage-debt.pdf.

———. "What Is a Debt-to-Income Ratio? Why Is the 43% Debt-to-Income
Ratio Important?" Updated March 3, 2017. https://www.consumerfinance
.gov/ask-cfpb/what-is-a-debt-to-income-ratio-why-is-the-43-debt-to
-income-ratio-important-en-1791/.

Consumer Reports. "Make Your Car Last 200,000 Miles." Updated May
9, 2017. https://www.consumerreports.org/car-repair-maintenance/
make-your-car-last-200-000-miles/.

Council for Disability Awareness. "Chances of Disability." Updated March 28, 2018. http://disabilitycanhappen.org/disability-statistic/.

Council for Economic Education. *Survey of the States: Economic and Personal Finance Education in Our Nation's Schools 2016.* New York: Council for Economic Education, 2016.

Cubanski, Juliette, Kendal Orgera, Anthony Damico, and Tricia Neuman. "How Many Seniors Are Living in Poverty? National and State Estimates Under the Official and Supplemental Poverty Measures in 2016." Kaiser Family Foundation. March 2, 2018. http://kff.org/report-section/poverty-among-seniors-issue-brief/.

Cubanski, Juliette, Christina Swoope, Anthony Damico, and Tricia Neuman. "How Much Is Enough? Out-of-Pocket Spending among Medicare Beneficiaries: A Chartbook." Kaiser Family Foundation. July 21, 2014. https://www.kff.org/medicare/report/how-much-is-enough-out-of-pocket-spending-among-medicare-beneficiaries-a-chartbook/.

Dahl, Corey, Brian Anderson, and Brian Gilbert. "The Shocking Statistics Behind the Life Insurance Coverage Gap." ThinkAdvisor. August 30, 2013. https://www.thinkadvisor.com/2013/08/30/the-shocking-statistics-behind-the-life-insurance/?slreturn=20180908182610.

Dale, Stacy Berg, and Alan B. Krueger. "Estimating the Payoff to Attending a More Selective College: An Application of Selection on Observables and Unobservables." Working Paper No. 7322, National Bureau of Economic Research, Cambridge, MA, August 1999. http://www.nber.org/papers/w7322.

DataHub. "US Investor Flow of Funds into Investment Classes (Bonds, Equities etc)." Accessed December 19, 2017. https://datahub.io/core/investor-flow-of-funds-us#data.

Delisle, Jason. *The Graduate Student Debt Review: The State of Graduate Student Borrowing.* New America Education Policy Program. March 2014. https://static.newamerica.org/attachments/750-the-graduate-student-debt-review/GradStudentDebtReview-Delisle-Final.pdf.

DeNavas-Walt, Carmen, and Bernadette D. Proctor. *Income and Poverty in the United States: 2014.* US Census Bureau Current Population Reports, P60-252. Washington, DC: US Government Printing Office, 2015.

DePillis, Lydia. "Why Age Discrimination Is Worse for Women." *Washington Post*, October 26, 2015. https://www.washingtonpost.com/news/wonk

/wp/2015/10/26/why-age-discrimination-is-worse-for-women/?utm
_term=.fc94f33fbe36.

Doyle, Alison. "How Often Do People Change Jobs?" *The Balance Careers*,
updated January 24, 2018. https://www.thebalancecareers.com/how
-often-do-people-change-jobs-2060467.

Duhigg, Charles. *The Power of Habit: Why We Do What We Do in Life and in
Business.* New York: Random House, 2012.

Dworak-Fisher, Keenan. "Access to Specific Provision of Employer Provided
Benefits: New Estimates." *Beyond the Numbers: Pay & Benefits* 4, no. 12
(September 2015). https://www.bls.gov/opub/btn/volume-4/access-to
-specific-provisions-of-employer-provided-benefits.htm.

Ecole Polytechnique Fédérale de Lausanne. "How Stress Tears Us Apart:
Enzyme Attacks Synaptic Molecule, Leading to Cognitive Impairment."
ScienceDaily, September 18, 2014. https://www.sciencedaily.com/releases
/2014/09/140918091418.htm.

Economides, Steve, and Annette Economides. *America's Cheapest Family Gets
You Right on the Money.* New York: Three Rivers, 2007.

Edvisors. "Interest Rates and Fees on Federal Student Loans." Accessed
October 2017. https://www.edvisors.com/college-loans/federal/stafford
/interest-rates/.

Eisenberg, Lee. *The Number: A Completely Different Way to Think about the Rest
of Your Life.* New York: Free Press, 2006.

Employee Benefit Research Institute. "Retirement Income Adequacy." Chap. 14
in *EBRI Databook on Employee Benefits 2014.* Updated July 2014. http://www
.ebri.org/pdf/publications/books/databook/DB.Chapter%2014.pdf (page
discontinued).

El Issa, Erin. "NerdWallet's 2017 American Household Credit Card Debt Study." 2017.
https://www.nerdwallet.com/blog/average-credit-card-debt-household/.

Farnham, Alan. "Public Pensions Face Underfunding Crisis." ABC
News. December 13, 2010. http://abcnews.go.com/Business/city
-pensions-americas-50-biggest-municipal-pension-shortfalls
/story?id=12366160.

Federal Reserve. "Consumer Credit—G.19." Q4 2017. https://www.federalre
serve.gov/releases/g19/current/.

Federal Student Aid. "Discharge Due to Death." Accessed December 2017.
https://studentaid.ed.gov/sa/repay-loans/forgiveness-cancellation/death.

————. "Interest Rates and Fees." Accessed November 2017. https://student aid.ed.gov/sa/types/loans/interest-rates.

————. "Repayment Plans." Accessed October 20, 2017. https://studentaid .ed.gov/sa/repay-loans/understand/plans.

Financial Engines. *Missing Out: How Much Employer 401(k) Matching Contributions Do Employees Leave on the Table?* May 2015. https://financial engines.com/docs/financial-engines-401k-match-report-050615.pdf.

FINRA Investor Education Foundation. *Financial Capability in the United States 2016*. Washington, DC: FINRA Investor Education Foundation, July 2016. http://www.usfinancialcapability.org/downloads/NFCS_2015_Report _Natl_Findings.pdf

FPA Research and Practice Institute. *Financial Planning in 2015: Today's Demands, Tomorrow's Challenges.* 2015. https://www.onefpa.org/business -success/ResearchandPracticeInstitute/Documents/RPI-2015_Trends-In -Financial-Planning_10-15-15.pdf.

Gilbride, Timothy J., Jeffrey Inman, and Karen M. Stilley. *What Determines Unplanned Purchases?: A Model Including Shopper Purchase History and Within-Trip Dynamics.* Philadelphia: Wharton School of Business, 2013.

Gist, John, and Carlos Figueiredo. "In Their Dreams: What Will Boomers Inherit?" AARP. June 2006. https://www.aarp.org/money/estate-planning /info-2006/dd139_inherit_1.html.

Gist, John and Megan Hatch. *Retirement Security Across Generations: Are Americans Prepared for Their Golden Years?* Washington, DC: The Pew Charitable Trusts, May 2013. http://www.pewtrusts.org/~/media/legacy /uploadedfiles/pcs_assets/2013/empretirementv4051013finalforwebpdf.pdf.

Graves, Ben. "2018 ACA Out-of-Pocket Maximums and Health Savings Account Limits." Hays Companies. May 12, 2017. http://www.hayscompanies .com/2018-aca-out-of-pocket-maximums-and-health-savings-account-limits/.

Greeley, Brendan. "U.S. Homeowners Are Repeating Their Mistakes." *Bloomberg,* February 14, 2013. http://www.bloomberg.com/bw /articles/2013-02-14/u-dot-s-dot-homeowners-are-repeating-their-mistakes.

Gunders, Dana. *Wasted: How America Is Losing Up to 40 Percent of Its Food from Farm to Fork to Landfill.* National Resources Defense Council Issue Paper 12-06-B. August 2012. https://www.nrdc.org/sites/default/files/wasted -food-IP.pdf.

Hershfield, Hal E., M. Tess Garton, Kacey Ballard, Gregory R. Samanez-Larkin, and Brian Knutson. "Don't Stop Thinking about Tomorrow: Individual Differences in Future Self Continuity Account for Saving." *Judgment and Decision Making* 4, no. 4 (June 2009): 280–86.

Hershfield, Hal E., Daniel G. Goldstein, William F. Sharpe, Jesse Fox, Leo Yeykelis, Laura L. Carstensen, and Jeremy N. Bailenson. "Increased Saving Behavior through Age-Progressed Renderings of the Future Self." *Journal of Marketing Research* 48 (2011): S23–S37.

Helman, Ruth, Craig Copeland, and Jack VanDerhei. "The 2015 Retirement Confidence Survey: Having a Retirement Savings Plan a Key Factor in Americans' Retirement Confidence." *EBRI Issue Brief*, no. 413 (April 2015).

Hirshbein, Laura Davidow. "William Osler and The Fixed Period: Conflicting Medical and Popular Ideas about Old Age." *Archives of Internal Medicine* 161, no. 17 (September 24, 2001). https://deepblue.lib.umich.edu/bitstream /handle/2027.42/83267/LDH%20Osler.pdf;sequence=1.

HomeAdvisor. "How Much Does It Cost to Remodel a Kitchen?" Accessed August 5, 2018. http://www.homeadvisor.com/cost/kitchens/remodel-a-kitchen/.

Huddleston, Cameron. "69% of Americans Have Less than $1,000 in Savings". September 19, 2016. https://www.gobankingrates.com/saving-money /savings-advice/data-americans-savings/.

The Institute for College Access and Success. "Project on Student Debt." Accessed July 27, 2018. http://ticas.org/posd/home.

———. "State Summary." 2017. https://ticas.org/posd/map-state -data#overlay=posd/state-summary/2017.

Internal Revenue Service. "Filing Season Statistics for Week Ending December 25, 2015." Updated May 2018. https://www.irs.gov/uac/newsroom /filing-season-statistics-for-week-ending-december-25-2015.

———. "Publication 590-B (2017), Distributions from Individual Retirement Arrangements (IRAs)." Updated February 21, 2018. https://www.irs.gov /publications/p590b/ch02.html.

Investment Company Institute. *2017 Investment Company Fact Book*. 57th ed. https://www.ici.org/pdf/2017_factbook.pdf.

Jacobson, Jeremy. "Start Here." 2016. http://www.gocurrycracker.com /start-here/.

Johnson, Steven Ross. "Financing Questions Loom as Private LTC Insurers Falter." *Modern Healthcare*, January 17, 2015. http://www.modernhealthcare .com/article/20150117/MAGAZINE/301179971.

Jones, Jeffrey M. "Majority in U.S. Do Not Have a Will." Gallup. May 18, 2016. http://www.gallup.com/poll/191651/majority-not.aspx.

Kadlec, Dan. "What Savings Rate You Need When Starting at Age 15, 25, 35 and 50." *Time*, September 28, 2012. http://business.time.com/2012/09/28/what -savings-rate-you-need-when-starting-at-age-15-25-35-and-50/.

Kilroy, Meaghan. "Target-Date-Fund Fees Fall for Ninth Consecutive Year." *Investment News*, May 8, 2018. http://www.investmentnews .com/article/20180508/FREE/180509928/target-date-fund-fees-fall -for-ninth-consecutive-year.

Kinnel, Russel. *Predictive Power of Fees: Why Mutual Fund Fees Are So Important*. Morningstar. May 4, 2016. http://corporate1.morningstar.com /ResearchArticle.aspx?documentId=752589.

Krejca, David. "How Many Stocks Make Up a Well-Diversified Portfolio?" *Seeking Alpha*, September 16, 2016. https://seekingalpha.com /article/4006697-many-stocks-make-well-diversified-portfolio.

Lewerer, Greg. "Car Depreciation: How Much Have You Lost?" February 14, 2014. Updated May 14, 2018. https://www.trustedchoice.com /insurance-articles/wheels-wings-motors/car-depreciation/.

Lunt, Peter K., and Sonia M. Livingstone. "Psychological, Social and Economic Determinants of Saving: Comparing Recurrent and Total Savings." *Journal of Economic Psychology* 12, no. 4 (1991): 621–41.

Ma, Jennifer, Sandy Baum, Matea Pender, and D'Wayne Bell. *Trends in College Pricing*. College Board. 2015. https://trends.collegeboard.org/sites/default /files/2015-trends-college-pricing-final-508.pdf.

Magloff, Lisa. "The Average Cost for Divorce." LegalZoom. Accessed September 2016. http://info.legalzoom.com/average-cost-divorce-20103.html.

Marum, Anna. "We Compared Prices at 7 Different Grocery Stores and the Results Surprised Us (interactive graphic)." *Oregonian*, Updated March 15, 2015. http://www.oregonlive.com/window-shop/index.ssf/2015/03/we _compared_prices_at_7_differ.html.

Maye, Michael. "Average Investor 20 Year Return Astoundingly Awful." *TheStreet*, July 18, 2012. https://www.thestreet.com/story/11621555/1 /average-investor-20-year-return-astoundingly-awful.html.

McCurry, Justin. "Early Retirement at 33." *Root of Good*, September 25, 2013. http://rootofgood.com/early-retirement-at-33-an-overview/.

Mackenzie, Sandy. "Determining Whether 401(k) Plan Fees Are Reasonable:

Are Disclosure Requirements Adequate?" *Insight on the Issues* 8. AARP Public Policy Institute. September 2008. http://assets.aarp.org/rgcenter/econ /i8_fees.pdf.

McKeon, Brigid. *Effective Sex Education*. Washington, DC: Advocates for Youth, 2006. http://www.advocatesforyouth.org/component/content /article/450-effective-sex-education (page discontinued).

MFS Fund Distributors Inc. "Emotion Drives Investor Decisions." Accessed February 2017. https://www.mfs.com/wps/FileServer Servlet?articleId=templatedata/internet/file/data/sales_tools /mfsp_bllbear_fly&servletCommand=default.

Miller, Claire Cain. "The Divorce Surge Is Over, but the Myth Lives On." *New York Times*, December 2, 2014. http://www.nytimes.com/2014/12/02/up shot/the-divorce-surge-is-over-but-the-myth-lives-on.html.

Morningstar. *The Morningstar Category Classifications*. April 29, 2016. http://mor ningstardirect.morningstar.com/clientcomm/Morningstar_Categories_US _April_2016.pdf.

Munnel, Alicia H., Jean-Pierre Aubry, Carolyn V. Crawford. *Investment Returns: Defined Benefit vs Defined Contribution Plans*. Center for Retirement Research Boston College. December 2015. http://crr.bc.edu/wp-content /uploads/2015/12/IB_15-21.pdf.

National Association of Insurance Commissioners. *A Shopper's Guide to Long-Term Care Insurance*. Revised 2013. https://www.ltcfeds.com/epassets /documents/naic_shoppers_guide.pdf.

National Bureau of Economic Research. "Borrowing from 401(k)s." *Bulletin on Aging and Health*, no. 2 (2015). http://www.nber.org/aginghealth/2015no2 /w21102.html.

O'Connor, Richard. *Rewire: Change Your Brain to Break Bad Habits, Overcome Addictions, Conquer Self-Destructive Behavior*. New York: Penguin, 2014.

Organisation for Economic Co-operation and Development. "Better Life Index—United States." Accessed 2015. http://www.oecdbetterlifeindex .org/topics/health/.

———. "Household Savings Forecasts." Indicator. Accessed September 2, 2016. https://data.oecd.org/hha/household-savings-forecast.htm.

Ortman, Jennifer, Victoria A. Velkoff, and Howard Hogan. M. *An Aging Nation: The Older Population in the United States*. Washington, DC: US Census Bureau, 2014.

Page, Ashley. "They Ain't Got No Money in the Bank: Celebrities Who Have Gone Bankrupt." *MadameNoire*, May 31, 2013. http://madamenoire .com/278370/they-aint-got-not-money-in-the-bank-celebrities-who-have -gone-bankrupt/9/.

Peckham, Carol. *Physician Debt and Net Worth Report*. April 29, 2015. https://www.medscape.com/features/slideshow/compensation/2015 /debt-and-net-worth.

The Pew Charitable Trusts. *Who's In, Who's Out: A Look at Employer-based Retirement Plans and Participation in the States*. January 2016. http://www .pewtrusts.org/~/media/assets/2016/01/retirement_savings_report_jan16.pdf.

PureWow. "How Realistic Are TV Characters' New York Apartments?" *Huffington Post*, October 25, 2013. Updated December 6, 2017. https://www .huffingtonpost.com/purewow/how-realistic-are-tv-char_b_4163843.html.

Queen, Karen Haywood. "Minimum Payment Survey: How Much Your Issuer Charges." Creditcards.com. Updated April 10, 2017. https://www.creditcards .com/credit-card-news/minimum-credit_card-payments-survey-1276.php.

Rho, Hye Jin. *Hard Work? Patterns in Physically Demanding Labor Among Older Workers*. Washington, DC: Center for Economic Policy and Research, August 2010. http://cepr.net/documents/publications/older-workers-2010-08.pdf.

Roberts, Dexter. "The Chinese Can't Kick Their Savings Habit." *Bloomberg Businessweek*, April 30, 2015. https://www.bloom berg.com/news/articles/2015-05-01/chinese-consumers-cling -to-saving-suppressing-spending.

Robinson, Mark. "Success of Auto Enrollment and Auto Increase: Using Behavioral Finance to Improve Retirement Planning." Presentation at the EBRI Policy Forum, Washington, DC, May 13, 2010. https://www.ebri.org /pdf/programs/policyforums/Robinson0510PF.pdf (page discontinued).

Rocha, Carrie. *Pocket Your Dollars: 5 Attitude Changes That Will Help You Pay Down Debt, Avoid Financial Stress, and Keep More of What You Make*. Bloomington, MN: Bethany House, 2013.

Rogers, Todd, Katherine L. Milkman, Leslie K. John, and Michael I. Norton. "Beyond Good Intentions: Prompting People to Make Plans Improves Follow-Through on Important Tasks." *Behavioral Science and Policy* 1, no. 2 (December 2015). http://scholar.harvard.edu/files/todd_rogers/files /beyond_good.pdf.

Rubin, Larry, Kevin Crowe, Adam Fisher, Omar Ghaznawi, Richard McCoach,

Rachel Narva, David Schaulewicz, Thomas Sullivan, and Toby White. *An Overview of the U.S. Long-Term Care Insurance Market (Past and Present): The Economic Need for LTC Insurance, the History of LTC Regulation and Taxation, and the Development of LTC Product Design Features.* Society of Actuaries. 2014. https://www.soa.org/essays-monographs /mono-2014-managing-ltc/.

Sallie Mae. "How America Saves for College." Infographic. 2015. https://www .salliemae.com/assets/Core/plan-for-college/how-america-saves-info graphic.pdf.

Sanburn, Josh. "So...Where'd All That Money Go?" *Time*, February 14, 2012. http://business.time.com/2012/02/16/top-9-celebrity-bankruptcies/.

Sass, Stephen A., and Jorge D. Ramos-Mercado. *Are Americans of All Ages and Incomes Shortsighted about Their Finances?* Trustees of Boston College, Center for Retirement Research. May 2015. http://crr.bc.edu/wp-content /uploads/2015/05/IB_15-9.pdf.

Saving for College. "Does a 529 Plan Affect Financial Aid?" Updated August 29, 2018. http://www.savingforcollege.com/intro_to_529s/does-a-529-plan -affect-financial-aid.php.

———. "Name the Top 7 Benefits of 529 Plans." Updated August 29, 2018. http://www.savingforcollege.com/intro_to_529s/name-the-top-7-benefits -of-529-plans.php.

The SCAN Foundation. *Who Pays for Long-Term Care in the U.S.?* The SCAN Foundation fact sheet. January 2013. https://www.thescanfoundation.org /sites/default/files/who_pays_for_ltc_us_jan_2013_fs.pdf.

Schieber, Sylvester J. *The Predictable Surprise: The Unraveling of the US Retirement System.* New York: Oxford University Press, 2012.

Schmeiser, Maximilian, Christiana Stoddard, and Carly Urban. "Does Salient Financial Information Affect Academic Performance and Borrowing Behavior among College Students?" Finance and Economics Discussion Series 2015-075. Washington, DC: Board of Governors of the Federal Reserve System, 2015. https://www.federalreserve.gov/econresdata/feds/2015/files /2015075pap.pdf.

Schwartz, Barry. *The Paradox of Choice: Why More Is Less.* New York: HarperCollins, 2004.

Scitovsky, Tibor. *The Joyless Economy: The Psychology of Human Satisfaction.* Rev. ed. New York: Oxford University Press, 1992.

Scott, Nate. "The 50 Greatest Yogi Berra Quotes." *For the Win*, September 23, 2015. https://ftw.usatoday.com/2015/09/the-50-greatest-yogi-berra-quotes.

Shiller, Robert, and Carl Kase. "U.S. Stock Markets 1871–Present and CAPE Ratio." Spreadsheet hosted by the Yale University Department of Economics. Accessed February 2017. http://www.econ.yale.edu/~shiller/data.htm.

Skolnik, Alfred M. "Private Pension Plans, 1950–1974." *Social Security Bulletin*, June 1976.

Social Security Administration. "Benefits Planner: Life Expectancy." Accessed August 27, 2018. https://www.ssa.gov/planners/lifeexpectancy.html.

———. "Life Expectancy Table." Accessed October 8, 2018.

———. "Benefit Calculator: Social Security Quick Calculator." Last modified May 27, 2014. https://www.ssa.gov/OACT/quickcalc/.

Social Security and Medicare Boards of Trustees. "A Summary of the 2015 Annual Reports." 2015. https://www.ssa.gov/oact/TRSUM/2015/index.html.

Stanley, Thomas J., and William D. Danko. *The Millionaire Next Door*. New York: RosettaBooks, 2010.

Statistic Brain. "Gym Membership Market Analysis." Accessed December 1, 2015. Updated May 30, 2018. http://www.statisticbrain.com/gym-membership-statistics/.

———. "Self Storage Industry Statistics." September 4, 2016. http://www.statisticbrain.com/self-storage-industry-statistics/.

Steindl-Rast, David. "Want to Be Happy? Be Grateful." Filmed June 2013. TED video, 14:27. https://www.ted.com/talks/david_steindl_rast_want_to_be_happy_be_grateful?language=en.

Steyer, Robert. "Cost, Complexity Cited for Lackluster Use of Managed Accounts." *Pensions and Investments*, January 25, 2016. http://www.pionline.com/article/20160125/PRINT/301259987/cost-complexity-cited-for-the-lackluster-use-of-managed-accounts.

Target Date Analytics. "A Brief History of Target Date Funds." January 2011. http://www.ucs-edu.net/cms/wp-content/uploads/2014/04/I_ABriefHistoryOfTargetDateFunds.pdf.

Taylor, Andrea Browne. "5 Things Home Improvement Reality TV Shows Don't Tell You." *Kiplinger*, October 16, 2014. https://www.kiplinger.com/slideshow/real-estate/T010-S001-what-home-improvement-shows-do-not-tell-you/index.html.

Taylor, Paul, project director. *The Return of the Multi-Generational*

Household. Pew Research Center Social and Demographic Trends Report. March 18, 2010. http://www.pewsocialtrends.org/2010/03/18/the-return-of-the-multi-generational-family-household/.

Thaler, Richard H., and Cass R. Sunstein. *Nudge: Improving Decisions about Health, Wealth, and Happiness.* New Haven, CT: Yale University Press, 2008.

TIAA-Cref. *Are Your Employees Borrowing from Their Futures?* June 2014. https://www.tiaa.org/public/pdf/C17504_Are_your_employees_borrowing_from_their_futures.pdf.

T. Rowe Price. *First Look: Assessing the New Retiree Experience.* July 29, 2014. https://www3.troweprice.com/usrps/content/dam/troweplan/pdfs/rfa/AssessingtheNewRetireeExperience_Artilcle.pdf.

Tuchman, Mitch. "Burt Malkiel on Active Management's Big Miss." Rebalance IRA. November 14, 2014. https://www.rebalance-ira.com/burt-malkiel-active-managements-big-miss/.

U.S. Bank. *2016 U.S. Bank Parent Financial Survey: Examining Financial Attitudes of Parent of Undergraduate Students.* 2016. https://stories.usbank.com/dam/Documents/ParentFinancialEducationReport.pdf.

US Bureau of Economic Analysis. "Personal Savings as a Percentage of Disposable Income." FRED Economic Data. Updated July 27, 2018. https://fred.stlouisfed.org/series/A072RC1Q156SBEA.

US Bureau of Labor Statistics. "Civilian Labor Force Participation Rate by Age, Sex, Race, and Ethnicity." October 2017. https://www.bls.gov/emp/tables/civilian-labor-force-participation-rate.htm.

———. "Consumer Expenditures—2016." Press release. August 29, 2017. http://www.bls.gov/news.release/cesan.nr0.htm.

———. "Consumer Price Index, U.S. City Average." Accessed March 2016. https://www.bls.gov/regions/midwest/data/consumerpriceindexhistorical_us_table.pdf.

———. "Employment, Hours, and Earnings from the Current Employment Statistics Survey (National)." Accessed February 8, 2017. https://data.bls.gov/timeseries/CES0000000001.

———. "Workers with Disability Insurance Plans." *The Economics Daily,* March 4, 2015. http://www.bls.gov/opub/ted/2015/disability-insurance-plans-for-workers.htm.

US Census Bureau. *Selected Characteristics of Households by Total Money Income: 2014.* 2015. https://www.census.gov/data/tables/time-series/demo/income -poverty/cps-hinc/hinc-01.2014.html.

US Department of Agriculture. "Food Prices and Spending." Updated July 25, 2018. http://www.ers.usda.gov/data-products/ag-and-food-statistics-chart ing-the-essentials/food-prices-and-spending.aspx.

US Department of Education. "Income-Driven Plans." Accessed February 2016. https://studentaid.ed.gov/sa/repay-loans/understand/plans/income-driven.

US Department of the Treasury. "HQM Corporate Bond Yield Curve Par Yields, 1984–Present." Excel spreadsheet. Accessed February 2016. https://www .treasury.gov/resource-center/economic-policy/corp-bond-yield.

US Department of Transportation, Federal Highway Administration. "Average Annual Miles per Driver by Age Group." Accessed July 13, 2016. Updated March 29, 2018. https://www.fhwa.dot.gov/ohim/onh00/bar8.htm.

Value Penguin. "Average Auto Loan Interest Rates: 2018 Facts and Figures." Accessed August 5, 2018. https://www.valuepenguin.com/auto-loans /average-auto-loan-interest-rates.

VanDerhei, Jack. "How Does the Probability of a 'Successful' Retirement Differ Between Participants in Final-Average Defined Benefit Plans and Voluntary Enrollment 401(k) Plans?" *EBRI Notes* 36, no. 10 (October 2015). https://www.ebri.org/pdf/notespdf/Notes.Oct15..DB-DC-only|. pdf (page discontinued).

VanDerhei, Jack, Sarah Holden, Luis Alonso, and Steven Bass. "401(k) Plan Asset Allocation, Account Balances, and Loan Activity in 2014." *EBRI Issue Brief*, no. 423 (April 2016). https://www.ebri.org/pdf/briefspdf/EBRI _IB_423.Apr16.401k-Update.pdf (page discontinued).

Vanguard. "How America Saves 2017: Vanguard 2016 Defined Contribution Plan Data". 2017. https://pressroom.vanguard.com/nonindexed/How-America -Saves-2017.pdf.

———. "Vanguard S&P 500 ETF (VOO)." Accessed October 8, 2018. https://in vestor.vanguard.com/etf/profile/voo.

———. "Vanguard 500 Admiral Shares (VFIAX)." Accessed October 8, 2018. https://investor.vanguard.com/mutual-funds/profile/vfiax.

———. "Vanguard 500 Investor Shares (VFINX)." Accessed October 8, 2018. https://investor.vanguard.com/mutual-funds/profile/vfinx.

Vilorio, Dennis. "Data on Display: Education Matters." US Bureau of

Labor Statistics Career Outlook. March 2016. https://www.bls.gov /careeroutlook/2016/data-on-display/education-matters.htm.

Weaver, Carolyn L. "Support of the Elderly before the Depression: Individual and Collective Arrangements." *Cato Journal* 7, no. 2 (Fall 1987). 503-525.

Wiatrowski, William J. "The Last Private Industry Pension Plans: A Visual Essay." *Monthly Labor Review*, December 2012. https://www.bls.gov/opub /mlr/2012/12/art1full.pdf.

Wolff, Edward N., and Maury Gittleman. "Inheritances and the Distribution of Wealth or Whatever Happened to the Great Inheritance Boom?" Working paper no. 445, Bureau of Labor Statistics, Washington, DC, January 2011.

Wolff-Mann, Ethan. "The Average American Is in Credit Card Debt, No Matter the Economy." *Money*, February 9, 2016. http://time.com/money/4213757 /average-american-credit-card-debt/.

Woolley, Suzanne. "How a Harvard Economist Screwed Up—and Then Saved—Her Retirement." *Bloomberg*, July 16, 2015. https://www .bloomberg.com/news/articles/2015-07-16/how-a-harvard-economist -screwed-up-and-then-saved-her-retirement.

Yahoo Finance. "S&P 500 Total Return Index." Accessed December 19, 2017. https://finance.yahoo.com/chart/%5ESP500TR.

Zagat. "The State of American Dining in 2015: How Foodies Feel about Tipping, Trendy Foods and More." January 20, 2015. https://www.zagat.com/b /the-state-of-american-dining-in-2015.

About the Author

JULIE GRANDSTAFF IS A VETERAN OF THE FINANCIAL SERVICES industry. In her career of more than twenty-five years, she managed a mutual fund and the fixed-income portfolio for a mid-sized insurance company, oversaw the investment selection for thousands of company retirement plans, developed a financial planning business, and managed the annuity business for that same insurer. She has a master's degree in finance and holds the Chartered Financial Analyst (CFA) designation.

Through diligent planning and saving, Julie and her husband, Jeff, were able to retire more than a decade early, at the ages of fifty-one and fifty-five, respectively. She volunteers her time managing the finances for a small theater company and serving on the investment committee for a local university. When she's not simply enjoying the freedom of not having to work, she spends her time educating others on how to plan and save for their financial futures through her blog at www.juliegrandstaff.com, one-on-one, and in workshops. She and Jeff live in Portland, Oregon, with their daughter, Kaye.

CPSIA information can be obtained
at www.ICGtesting.com
Printed in the USA
LVHW081801060519
616797LV00029B/792/P